W9-DIT-980

Also by Thomas Verny

INSIDE GROUPS

The Secret

Thomas Verny, M.D.
with John Kelly

the

Life of Unborn Child

SUMMIT BOOKS NEW YORK

Copyright © 1981 by Thomas Verny, M.D. and John Kelly
All rights reserved
including the right of reproduction
in whole or in part in any form
Published by SUMMIT BOOKS
A Simon & Schuster Division of Gulf & Western Corporation
Simon & Schuster Building
Rockefeller Center
1230 Avenue of the Americas
New York, New York 10020

SUMMIT BOOKS and colophon are trademarks of Simon & Schuster
Designed by Irving Perkins Associates
Manufactured in the United States of America
10 9 8 7 6 5 4 3 2 1

Library of Congress Cataloging in Publication Data
Verny, Thomas R.
    The secret life of the unborn child.

    Bibliography: p.
    Includes index.
    1. Fetus.   2. Prenatal influences.   3. Behavioral
embryology.   4. Maternal-fetal exchange.   5. Child-
birth—Psychological aspects.   I. Kelly, John, 1945–
II. Title.
RG600.V47   155.4′2   81-5626
                        AACR2
ISBN 0-671-25312-3
        0-671-25313-1 Pbk.

Acknowledgments

It would take a book in itself to thank all the investigators whose ideas and research have contributed to the making of this work. But, because they were so generous with their time and knowledge, I owe a special debt of gratitude to Dr. Peter Fedor-Freybergh, University Professor of Obstetrics and Gynecology at the University of Uppsala (Sweden); Dr. Alfred Tomatis, Professeur de Psycholinguistique at the École des Psychologues praticiens de l'Institut Catholique, Paris; Drs. Sepp Schindler and Igor Caruso, respectively Professor and Professor Emeritus of Psychology at the University of Salzburg (Austria); Dr. R. D. Laing of London; Dr. Michele Clements of the London Maternity Hospital; Sheila Kitzinger, advisor to England's National Childbirth Trust; Dr. Lewis Mehl of the Center for Research on Birth and Human Development, Berkeley, Cal.; Dr. Stanislav Grof, Esalen Institute, Big Sur, Cal.; Dr. David Cheek of San Francisco; Dr. Gustav Hans Graber of Bern, Switzerland; and Sigrid Enausten of the Max Planck Institute, Munich (Germany).

7

I would also like to thank my friend Sandra Collier for her constant support and wise counsel; Jonathan Segal, for his firm and thoughtful editorial guidance; and Anne Cohen, who turned my illegible scribblings into neatly typed pages. All my staff—Sandy Bogart, Geraldine Fogarty, Debbie Nixon, Nick Stephens and Shelley Owen —contributed immensely to this enterprise with their suggestions and clinical case material. I owe a special debt of thanks to Michael Owen, who helped in my research on the link between pregnancy, birth and personality; to Sheila Weller for her always insightful editorial ideas; to Natalie Rosen for sharing her extensive library and knowledge of midwifery with me; and to Naomi Bennett for her many creative ideas and comments.

Finally, I'd like to take this opportunity to express my gratitude to my patients, who trusted me enough to share their deepest feelings with me. They were the real inspiration for this book.

Thomas Verny
January 1981

Contents

Foreword

This book really began in the winter of 1975 during a weekend I spent with some friends at their cottage in the country. Helen, my hostess, was seven months pregnant and radiant. Often in the evenings I would find her sitting alone in front of the fireplace, softly singing a beautiful lullaby to her unborn child.

This touching scene left a deep impression on me, so when Helen told me later, after the birth of her son, that that lullaby had a magical effect on him, I was intrigued. It seemed that no matter how hard the baby was crying, when Helen began singing that song he quieted down. Was her experience unique, I wondered, or did a woman's actions, perhaps even her thoughts and feelings, influence her unborn child?

I already knew, of course, that at one time or another nearly every expectant mother senses that she and her unborn child are reacting to one another's feelings. And like most psychiatrists I'd heard stories and dreams from my patients that seemed to make sense only in terms of prenatal and birth experiences. Now I began to pay special attention to those recollections.

I also started searching the scientific literature for information that would help me to understand the mind of the unborn and newborn child for, by this time, I was convinced that he indeed had a mind. I was encouraged by the studies of Dr. Lester Sontag, which demonstrated that maternal attitudes and feelings could leave a permanent mark on an unborn child's personality—but his work was carried out in the 1930s and '40s. Most of the new and truly exciting research I discovered was in such related fields as neurology and physiology. Utilizing a new generation of medical technology, which became available in the late 1960s and early '70s, investigators in these and other specialties were finally able to study the child, undisturbed, in his natural habitat. What they found added up to a dramatically different picture of fetal life. Thanks in part to all of them, I have been able to present here a fundamentally new portrait of the unborn child, one that is very different from the passive, mindless creature of the traditional pediatrics texts.

We now know that the unborn child is an aware, reacting human being who from the sixth month on (and perhaps even earlier) leads an active emotional life. Along with this startling finding we have made these discoveries:

• The fetus can see, hear, experience, taste and, on a primitive level, even learn *in utero* (that is, in the uterus —before birth). Most importantly, he can *feel*—not with an adult's sophistication, but feel nonetheless.

• A corollary to this discovery is that what a child feels and perceives begins shaping his attitudes and expectations about himself. Whether he ultimately sees himself and, hence, acts as a happy or sad, aggressive or meek, secure or anxiety-ridden person depends, in part, on the messages he gets about himself in the womb.

• The chief source of those shaping messages is the child's mother. *This does not mean every fleeting worry, doubt or anxiety a woman has rebounds on her child.* What matters are deep persistent *patterns* of feeling. Chronic anxiety or a wrenching ambivalence about motherhood can leave a deep scar on an unborn child's personality. On the other hand, such life-enhancing emotions as joy, elation and anticipation can contribute significantly to the emotional development of a healthy child.

• New research is also beginning to focus much more on the father's feelings. Until recently his emotions were disregarded. Our latest studies indicate that this view is dangerously wrong. They show that how a man feels about his wife and unborn child is one of the single most important factors in determining the success of a pregnancy.

This book is the product of six years of intensive study, thought, research and travel. In the process of assembling material that appears in it, I have visited London, Paris, Berlin, Nice, Rome, Basel, Salzburg, Vienna, New York, Boston, San Francisco, New Orleans and Honolulu in order to talk and exchange ideas with leading psychiatrists, psychologists, physiologists, fetologists, obstetricians and pediatricians. I have also conducted several research projects of my own—two of which are included in the book—and treated hundreds of patients affected by traumatic pregnancies or deliveries.

Because the unborn child you will meet in these pages is radically different from the being described in both the popular and the medical press, I felt it essential to the credibility of the ideas I am advancing that they be supported by stringent scientific reports and studies. I think you will find these make lively and fascinating reading in themselves. Necessarily some of the studies deal with the impact of negative maternal emotions—much of our new knowledge has been gained by studying the impact of these emotions. As is so often the case in medicine, we learn how and why things go right by first understanding how and why they go wrong.

The clinical investigators who have made these discoveries have generally been more interested in the theoretical side of their work than in its more practical application. That is not uncommon. But obviously those discoveries have enormous implications for parenting. With this new knowledge at their disposal, mothers and fathers have an unparalled opportunity to help shape the personality of their unborn child. They can actively contribute to his happiness and well-being, and not just in utero, nor in the years immediately following birth, but *for the rest of his life*. That realization led directly to the book you are holding.

Chapter One

The Secret Life
of the Unborn Child

This book is about many things—the origins of human consciousness, the growth and development of the unborn and newly born child—but principally it is about the shaping of the human mind, about how we become who we are. And it is based on the discovery that the unborn child is a *feeling, remembering, aware* being, and because he* is, what happens to him—what happens to all of us—in the nine months between conception and birth molds and shapes personality, drives and ambitions in very important ways.

This realization and the remarkable body of research it springs from take us well beyond what we know—or think we know—about the emotional development of the unborn child. And while, scientifically, that is enormously

* The pronoun "he" is used throughout this book solely to avoid reader confusion.

exciting (among other things, it forever displaces the old Freudian notion that personality does not begin forming until the second or third year), even more exciting is the way it deepens and enriches the meaning and importance of parenting, especially mothering. In fact, the single most gratifying aspect of our new knowledge is what it reveals about the pregnant woman and her role in shaping and guiding her unborn child's personality. Her tools are her thoughts and feelings, and with them she has the opportunity to create a human being favored with more advantages than previously thought possible.

I do not make the claim that everything that happens to her in these critical months irrevocably shapes her baby's future. Many things go into the molding of a new life. Maternal thoughts and feelings are just one element in the mix, but what makes them a unique element is that unlike givens such as genetic inheritance, they are controllable. *A woman can make them as positive a force as she wishes.* Most emphatically, that does not mean a child's future happiness hinges on his mother's ability to think bright thoughts twenty-four hours a day. Occasional doubts, ambivalences and anxieties are a normal part of pregnancy and, as we shall see later, may actually help an unborn baby's development. What it does mean is that an expectant or prospective mother now has at her disposal another way of actively affecting her baby's emotional development for the good.

Though one could use the word "breakthrough" to describe this realization, it has grown out of other recent findings. In the late 1960s, for instance, we discovered a post-birth system of mother–child communication called bonding. In many ways our new research is a logical extension of this earlier finding, since it moves the communication system back a step and places it in the womb. Medically, much the same is true: Considering what we have learned recently about the effects of maternal diet, drinking, and drug taking on the unborn child, and also about the role emotions play in sickness and health, it follows that a mother's thoughts and feelings would have a potentially beneficial effect upon her unborn child.

It also makes sense that our new knowledge would enhance the father's part in pregnancy. A relationship with a loving and sensitive man provides a woman with an ongoing system of emotional support during pregnancy. And if, in our ignorance, we have disrupted this delicate system by rudely excluding the man, now that we have discovered—or more accurately, rediscovered—just how important emotional security and nurturing are to a woman and to her unborn child, he can finally be restored to his rightful place in pregnancy.

These new ideas come directly out of laboratories in America, Canada, England, France, Sweden, Germany, Austria, New Zealand, and Switzerland, where for the past two decades investigators have been quietly and painstakingly assembling a dramatically new view of the fetus, of birth, of the beginning stages of life.

What you are reading is a first attempt to bring news of their revolutionary work to a wider public. Because it is a first attempt, some of what follows will necessarily be speculative, though I will attempt to separate what we know from what we only think we know. Inevitably, some of it will also be controversial. I do not expect everyone to agree with me on each and every point.

But I am convinced this book and, even more, this entire area of exploration is one of bright unbounding hope: hope for physicians because it will allow them to prevent many of the missed opportunities of pregnancy and birth, hope for mothers and fathers because it deepens and enriches the nature of parenting, and most of all, hope for the unborn child.

He is the chief beneficiary of our new knowledge. Far different, far more aware, responsive and loving than anyone had imagined, he deserves—in fact, requires—a more sensitive, nurturing, *humane* kind of care in the womb and at birth than he gets now. French obstetrician Frederick Leboyer, author of *Birth Without Violence*, sensed this intuitively, which is why he has argued so compellingly for more gentle birthing methods. What we have learned, clinically, confirms his views.

Providing the newborn with a warm, reassuring, humane environment does make a difference because the child is very much aware of how he is born. He senses gentleness, softness and a caring touch, and he responds to them much as he senses and responds in a quite different way to the bright lights, electrical beeps, and cold, impersonal atmosphere that are so often associated with a medical birth.

But this knowledge and the revolution it encompasses also go beyond Leboyer and beyond any single notion of childbearing; it throws open the unborn child's mind to us for the first time. Most remarkably, it reveals that he is conscious or aware, though his consciousness is not as deep or complex as an adult's. He is incapable of understanding the shades of meaning an adult can put into a simple word or gesture; but, as some new studies show (they will be discussed in more detail in the next chapter), he is sensitive to remarkably subtle emotional nuances. He can sense and react not only to large, undifferentiated emotions such as love and hate, but also to more shaded complex feeling states like ambivalence and ambiguity.

Precisely at what moment his brain cells acquire this ability is still unknown. One group of investigators believes something like consciousness exists from the very first moments of conception. As evidence, they point to the thousands of perfectly healthy women who repeatedly abort spontaneously. There is speculation that in the very first weeks—perhaps even hours—after conception, the fertilized ovum possesses enough self-awareness to sense rejection and enough will to act on it. This notion and the evidence to support it will be examined in more detail later. For now, as interesting as it is, this theory is just that, a theory, not proven fact.

Most of what is known with real authority—because it has been confirmed by physiological, neurological, biochemical, and psychological studies—is known about the child from the sixth month in utero onward. By almost any measure, he is a fascinating human being at this point. He can already remember, hear, even learn. The unborn child is, in fact, a very quick study, as a group of investigators demonstrated in what has come to be regarded as a classic report.

They taught sixteen unborn babies to respond to a vibrating sensation by kicking. Normally, an unborn child won't react that way to such a gentle sensation. He will ignore it, in fact. But, in this case, the investigators were able to create what behavioral psychologists call a conditioned or learned response in their young subjects by first exposing them several times to something that would make them kick naturally—a loud noise (it was made a few feet from each mother and her child's reaction was monitored by sensors strapped on her abdomen). Then the investigators introduced the vibration. Each child was exposed to it immediately after the noise was made near his mother. The researchers' assumption was that after enough exposures, eventually the association between vibration and kicking would become so automatic in the babies' minds that they would kick even when the vibration was used without the noise. And it proved correct. The vibration became their cue and their kicking in response to it a learned behavior.

This study, which provides a good glimpse of the unborn child's capabilities, also does more. It shows one of the ways personality characteristics and traits begin forming in utero. Our likes and dislikes, fears and phobias—in other words, all the distinct behaviors that make us uniquely ourselves—are, in part, also the product of conditioned learning. And as we have just seen, the womb is where this special kind of learning begins. To illustrate how it shapes future traits, let's consider the sensation of anxiety. What could produce the roots of a deep-seated, long-term anxiety in an unborn child? One possibility is his mother's smoking. In a remarkable study done several years ago, Dr. Michael Lieberman showed that an unborn child grows emotionally agitated (as measured by the quickening of his heartbeat) each time his mother thinks of having a cigarette. She doesn't even have to put it to her lips or light a match; just her *idea* of having a cigarette is enough to upset him. Naturally, the fetus has no way of knowing his mother is smoking—or thinking about it—but he is intellectually sophisticated enough to associate the experience of her smoking with the unpleasant sensation it produces in him. This is caused by the drop in his oxygen supply (smoking lowers the oxygen content of the maternal blood passing the placenta), which is physiologically harmful to him, but possibly even more harmful are the psychological effects of maternal smoking. It thrusts him into a chronic state of uncertainty and fear. He never knows when that unpleasant physical sensation will reoccur, or how painful it will be when it does, only that it will reoccur. And that's the kind of situation which does predispose toward a deep-seated, conditioned anxiety.

Another, happier kind of learning that goes on in utero is speech. Each of us has an idiosyncratic rhythm to our talk. Often, this is so muted that those around us don't notice it, but the difference always shows up on sound-analysis tests. Our speech patterns are as distinct as our fingerprints. The origins of these differences are no great mystery. They come from our mothers. We learn our speech by copying hers. Logically enough, scientists used to assume this copying didn't occur until well into infancy, but now many of them have come to agree with Dr. Henry Truby, professor of Pediatrics, Linguistics and Anthropology at the University of Miami, that this learning process begins earlier, in utero. As evidence, Dr. Truby points to recent studies which show the fetus hears clearly from the sixth month in utero, and, even more startling, that he moves his body rhythm to his mother's speech.

Considering his acute hearing, it should come as no surprise that the unborn child is also capable of learning a bit about music. A four- or five-month-old fetus definitely responds to sound and melody—and responds in very discriminating ways. Put Vivaldi on the phonograph and even the most agitated baby relaxes. Put Beethoven on and even the calmest child starts kicking and moving.

Of course, personality is much more than the sum of what we learn—in or out of the womb. My point is that since we have finally identified some of the early experiences which shape future traits and characteristics, a woman can now begin actively influencing her child's life well before birth. One way is by giving up, or cutting back on, cigarettes during pregnancy. Another way is by talking to the child. He really does hear; and, even more importantly, he responds to what he hears. Soft, soothing talk makes him feel loved and wanted. Not because he understands the words; obviously, they are well beyond his comprehension. But the tone of what is being said isn't. He is mature enough intellectually to sense the emotional tone of the maternal voice.

It's even possible to begin teaching an unborn baby. At the very least, a pregnant woman who spends a few minutes each day listening to soothing music could make her child feel more relaxed and tranquil. At most, that early exposure might create in the child a lifelong musical interest. It did for Boris Brott, conductor of the Hamilton (Ontario) Philharmonic Symphony.

One evening, a few years ago, I heard Brott interviewed on the radio. He is a colorful man with a gift for storytelling. On this particular night, he was being quizzed about opera; toward the end of the discussion, the interviewer asked him how he had become interested in music. It was a simple enough question—asked, I suspect, more to kill time than anything else—but it stopped Brott. He hesitated for a moment and said, "You know, this may sound strange, but music has been a part of me since before birth." Perplexed, the interviewer asked him to explain.

"Well," said Brott, "as a young man, I was mystified by this unusual ability I had—to play certain pieces sight unseen. I'd be conducting a score for the first time and, suddenly, the cello line would jump out at me; I'd know the flow of the piece even before I turned the page of the score. One day, I mentioned this to my mother, who is a professional cellist. I thought she'd be intrigued because it was always the cello line that was so distinct in my mind. She was; but when she heard what the pieces were, the mystery quickly solved itself. All the scores I knew sight unseen were ones she had played while she was pregnant with me."

A few years ago, at a conference, I encountered another example of prenatal learning that was not only as arresting as Brott's, but also supported Dr. Truby's notions about speech forming in utero. It came from a young American mother who had lived in Toronto during her pregnancy. One afternoon, she found her two-year-old daughter sitting on the living room floor chanting to herself, "Breathe in, breathe out, breathe in, breathe out." The woman said she recognized the words immediately; they were part of a Lamaze exercise. But how had her child picked them up? Her first thought was that the youngster had overheard them on television, but she quickly realized that was impossible. They lived in Oklahoma City, and any program about it her daughter would have seen would have been on the American version of Lamaze; those phrases are used only in the Canadian version. Since that was the one she had taken, there was only one possible explanation: Her daughter had overheard and memorized* the words while she was still in the womb.

* One of the problems with writing a book about the unborn child is that one is forced to use a vocabulary that is designed for adult mental states. Obviously, a fetus doesn't actively "memorize" the way we do. But, as we shall see later, memory traces do begin forming on the fetal brain by the sixth or seventh month, possibly earlier.

Not too long ago, a story like this or Brott's would have been fortunate to earn a footnote in a medical paper. But such incidents are now finally receiving the serious scientific consideration they deserve, due to the rise of an exciting new discipline called prenatal psychology. Centered primarily in Europe and drawing most of its practitioners from obstetrics, psychiatry and clinical psychology, the discipline is unique not only in the unusual nature of its subject matter, but also in the strong practical bent of its research. Indeed, in the short space of a decade since its creation, we have already learned enough about the unborn child's mind and emotions to help rescue thousands of youngsters from a lifetime of debilitating emotional disorders.

I say "we" because it was the promise of preventing such tragedies that led me into prenatal psychology. Over the years, in hospitals, while teaching and in my practice, I have seen hundreds of people who have been deeply scarred by destructive prenatal influences, patients whose afflictions can be explained only in terms of what happened to them in the womb and at birth. Nor is my experience unique; many of my fellow psychiatrists have treated similar cases. Prenatal psychology, it seems to me, finally offers a way of preventing many of these tragedies from occurring in the first place. Beyond this, we have a way of materially improving an entire generation's chances of entering life free of corrosive mental and emotional disorders that have beset youngsters in the past.

I am not suggesting that we have a universal panacea, which will magically banish our ills. Nor am I suggesting that every trivial emotional upset that touches us stretches back to the womb. Life is not static. What happens at twenty, at forty, even at sixty certainly influences and alters us. *But it is important to point out that events affect us quite differently in the first stages of life.* An adult, and to a lesser degree a child, has had time to develop defenses and responses. He can soften or deflect the impact of experience. An unborn child cannot. What affects him does so directly. That's why maternal emotions etch themselves so deeply on his psyche and why their tug remains so powerful later in life. Major personality characteristics seldom change. If optimism is engraved on the mind of an unborn child it will take a great deal of adversity later to erase it. Will this child be an artist or a mechanic, prefer Rembrandt to Cézanne, be left-handed or right-handed? All these fine details remain beyond current knowledge, and frankly I think it is just as well. To be able to predict very specific personality traits with absolute precision would take much of the mystery out of life.

Where our new knowledge can legitimately make a difference is in helping to identify and prevent the roots of serious personality problems. Most women know that to take care of themselves emotionally means automatically to take care of their unborn children. As scientists we have with our charts and studies confirmed that wisdom, but we have also gone beyond it. I believe our growing ability to spot, in utero, potentially troubling and disturbed behavior can be of immense benefit to thousands of yet-to-be-born children, to their parents and ultimately to society. To a small degree we have already begun exercising this ability, often with surprising results, as the following study illustrates.

The researchers began with the assumption that fetal activity is frequently an accurate sign of anxiety. If a child's behavior in the womb has any predictive meaning at all, they reasoned, the most active fetuses would one day grow into the most anxious youngsters. That is exactly what happened. The babies who moved around the most in utero grew into the most anxious children. They were not simply a bit more fretful than normal. They were bursting, bubbling over with anxiety. These two- and three-year-olds felt an almost heartbreaking discomfort in even the most common social situations. They shied away from their teachers, from their schoolmates, from making friends, and from all human contact. They were most comfortable, most relaxed and least anxious when they were alone.

How they will behave later on cannot be predicted with absolute certainty, of course. Perhaps a good marriage or a particularly rewarding career or parenthood or therapy or something or someone else will end up counteracting some of these anxieties. Yet it seems safe to say that most of those frightened youngsters will still be scurrying into corners to avoid encounters at thirty. The difference is that then they will be trying to avoid husbands, wives and their own children instead of teachers and playmates. The cycle will repeat itself.

It doesn't have to. If more pregnant women were to start communicating with their children it would represent a monumental beginning. Just imagine how you would feel alone in a room for six, seven, or eight months without any emotional or intellectual stimulation. That is, more or less, the net effect of ignoring an unborn child. Obviously his emotional and intellectual needs are far more primitive than ours. The important point is that he has them. He has to feel loved and wanted just as urgently—perhaps even more urgently—than we do. He has to be talked to and thought of; otherwise his spirit and often his body, too, begin wilting.

Studies on pregnant schizophrenic and psychotic women testify eloquently to the devastating effects of emotional neglect in utero. In these cases, the women simply cannot help it. The effects of mental disease make meaningful communication with their children impossible. But that silence or chaos often leaves deep scars on the youngsters. At birth they tend to have far more physical and emotional problems than the babies of mentally healthy women.*

In the following chapters, the question of how all this communication occurs will be examined. The point here is that it does—*and that we can do something about it.* To a certain extent, we can even measure its quality and directness. By and large, the personality of the unborn child a woman bears is a function of the quality of mother–child communication, and also of its specificity. If the communication was abundant, rich and, most important, nurturing, the chances are very good that the baby will be robust, healthy and happy.

This communication is an important part of bonding. And since every investigator who has studied bonding after birth agrees that it is immensely beneficial to both mother and child, it stands to reason that bonding before birth would be equally important. Indeed, I believe it to be far more beneficial. Life, even life in the first few minutes and hours, offers endless distractions—sights, sounds, smells and noises. Life in the womb, on the other

---

* There will always be people who will look for physical causes of emotional disturbances. However, after thousands of studies of schizophrenics and manic-depressives, no one chemical has been found in their blood systems the transfer of which would reproduce their symptoms.

hand, was much more constant, bounded completely by his mother and everything she has said, felt, thought and hoped. Even outside noises were conducted through her.

How can he not be profoundly affected by her? Even something as seemingly mundane and neutral as her heartbeat has an effect. Without question, it is an essential part of his life-support system. The child does not know that, of course; he only knows that the reassuring rhythm of its beat is one of the major constellations in his universe. He falls asleep to it, wakes to it, moves to it, rests to it. Because the human mind, even the human mind in utero, is a symbol-making entity, the fetus gradually attaches a metaphorical meaning to it. Its steady *thump-thump* comes to symbolize tranquillity, security and love to him. In its presence, he usually flourishes.

This was demonstrated a few years ago in a unique and ingenious study. It consisted merely of piping a tape of a human heartbeat into a nursery filled with newborn babies. The researchers assumed that if the maternal heartbeat had any emotional significance, the newborns in the nursery on the days it played would behave differently from the babies there on the days it did not. That is precisely what happened.

Except it happened in a much more conclusive way than had been expected. The scientists, fairly certain some differences would show up when they designed the study, were stunned by the number and magnitude of the ones that occurred. In virtually every way, the heartbeat babies did better, in most cases, much better. They ate more, weighed more, slept more, breathed better, cried less and got sick less. Not because they received special treatment or had superior parents or better doctors, but simply because they were exposed to a two-dollar tape recording of a heartbeat.

Of course, that's something a woman has no control over; her heartbeat operates, in a sense, on automatic pilot. But she can learn to understand her emotions and deal with them more effectively. And that's vital to the well-being of her child, because his mind is shaped by her thoughts and feelings in fundamental ways. Whether his mind evolves into something essentially hard, angular and dangerous or soft, flowing and open depends largely on whether her thoughts and emotions are positive and reinforcing or negative and etched with ambivalence.

This absolutely does not mean that occasional doubts and uncertainty will damage your child. Such feelings are natural and harmless. What I'm talking about is a clear-cut, continual pattern of behavior. Only that kind of intense ongoing emotion is capable of creating the kinds of conditioned learning that will negatively affect a child. A physically difficult birth with its attendant emotional strains does not change things. It is what you want and feel and communicate to the baby that matters.

This is why what a woman thinks about her child makes such an important difference. Her thoughts—her love or rejection, or ambivalence—begin defining and shaping his emotional life. What she creates are not specific traits such as extroversion or optimism or aggressiveness. These are largely adult words with adult meanings, too specific, too finely tuned to apply to the mind of a six-month-old unborn child.

What is forming are broader, more deeply rooted tendencies—such as a sense of security or self-esteem. From these, specific character traits develop later in childhood —as in those youngsters I mentioned earlier. They were not born shy. They were born *anxious*. Painful shyness may grow out of that anxiety.

A happier example is security. A secure person is

deeply self-confident. How can he not be when he has been told from the very edge of consciousness onward that he is wanted and loved? Such attributes as optimism, confidence, friendliness and extroversion flow naturally from that sense.

All these are precious things to give a child. And they can be given so easily: by creating a warm, emotionally enriching environment in utero, a woman can make a decisive difference in everything her child feels, hopes, dreams, thinks and accomplishes throughout life.

During these months, a woman is her baby's conduit to the world. Everything that affects her, affects him. And nothing affects her as deeply or hits with such lacerating impact as worries about her husband (or partner). Because of that, few things are more dangerous to a child, emotionally and physically, than a father who abuses or neglects his pregnant wife. Virtually everyone who has studied the expectant father's role—and, sadly, so far, only a handful of researchers have—has found that his support is absolutely essential to her and, thus, to their child's well-being.

That fact alone makes the man an important part of the prenatal equation. An equally vital factor in the child's emotional well-being is his father's commitment to the marriage. Any number of things can influence a man's ability to relate to his partner, from the way he feels about his wife or his own father to his job pressures or his own insecurities. (Ideally, of course, the time to work out these problems is before conceiving, not during a pregnancy.) But recent studies also indicate that what affects his sense of commitment most deeply—for better or worse—is when and if he begins bonding with his child.

For obvious physiological reasons, a man is at something of a disadvantage here. The child is not an organic part of him. But not all the physical impediments of pregnancy are insurmountable. Something as ordinary as talking is a good example: A child hears his father's voice in utero, and there is solid evidence that hearing that voice makes a big emotional difference. In cases where a man talked to his child in utero using short soothing words, the newborn was able to pick out his father's voice in a room even in the first hour or two of life. More than pick it out, he responds to it emotionally. If he's crying, for instance, he'll stop. That familiar, soothing sound tells him he is safe.

Bonding also directly influences the expectant father in more general ways. Stereotypes often portray him as well-meaning but bumbling. This creates an insidious crisis of confidence in many men. In defense, they tend to withdraw from their wives during pregnancy to the safety of friends and colleagues who provide them with respect and validation. Bonding is a way—a very important way—to break this damaging cycle and to involve the man much more deeply and meaningfully in his child's life from the very beginning. And the sooner he involves himself, the more his new son or daughter is likely to benefit.

This view of fathering is drastically new. In fact, most of what is in the pages that follow is new and some of it is frankly radical; radical in the original sense of that word —a sharp departure from past practices. But that and nothing less than that is necessary if we hope to produce future generations of increasingly healthy, emotionally secure children.

Chapter Two

The New Knowledge

As a professor of psycholinguistics* in Paris and author
of several highly regarded papers and books, Dr. Alfred
Tomatis knows the value of scientific data as well as anyone. But he also knows a story can sometimes make the
point more effectively and simply than a dozen studies.
So when he wants to illustrate the shaping power of prenatal experiences, he often tells the story of Odile, an
autistic child (a child who withdraws from reality) he
treated several years ago.

Like most youngsters with her affliction, Odile was virtually mute. When Dr. Tomatis first saw her in his office,
she neither spoke nor appeared to hear when spoken to.
At first Odile clung stubbornly to her silence. But slowly
Dr. Tomatis's treatment began drawing her out. Within
a month, she was listening and speaking. Naturally, her
parents were pleased with this progress; at the same time,

---

* At the École des Psychologues praticiens de l'Institut Catholique.

they were also a bit perplexed by it: They noticed their daughter's comprehension improved markedly whenever they spoke English instead of French. What perplexed them was where Odile had picked up her knowledge. Neither of them spoke much English at home and, until she came under Dr. Tomatis's care, four-year-old Odile had been almost totally impervious to the spoken word, no matter in what language it was uttered. Even assuming the unlikely, that she had somehow learned it by overhearing snippets of her parents' conversations, why hadn't any of her older (and normal) brothers and sisters done so as well?

Initially Dr. Tomatis found all this equally baffling, until one day when Odile's mother casually mentioned that through most of her pregnancy, she had worked in a Paris import-export firm where only English was spoken.

The realization that even the rudiments of a language may be laid down in the womb has taken us full circle. Forty years ago, such a notion would have been dismissed as impossible, while four hundred years ago, it would have been accepted as a matter of fact. Our ancestors were well aware that a mother's experiences impressed themselves on her unborn child. That's why the Chinese established the first prenatal clinics a thousand years ago. It is also why even the most primitive cultures have had strictures warning pregnant women away from frightening events, such as fires. Centuries of observation had shown them the powerful effects of maternal anxiety and fear.

References to these prenatal influences can be found in many ancient texts from Hippocrates' journals to the Bible. In one graphic passage from St. Luke (Luke 1:44), for instance, Elizabeth exclaims, "For lo, as soon as the voice of thy salutation sounded in my ears, the babe in my womb leaped for joy."

The first man to grasp the idea in all its dimensions, however, was neither a saint nor a physician, but the great Italian artist, inventor and genius Leonardo da Vinci. Leonardo's *Quaderni* has more to say about pre-natal influences than many of the most modern medical texts. In one especially insightful passage, he wrote: "the same soul governs the two bodies . . . the things desired by the mother are often found impressed on the child which the mother carries at the time of the desire . . . one will, one supreme desire, one fear that a mother has, or mental pain has more power over the child than over the mother, since frequently the child loses its life thereby."

The rest of us needed four centuries and help from another genius to catch up with Leonardo. In the eighteenth century man began his long, torturous love affair with the machine and the effects were felt everywhere, including medicine. Doctors looked at the human body pretty much the way children now look at Erector sets. Illness was simply a matter of finding out what went where and figuring out why what was supposed to go there didn't. What mattered was what could be immediately seen, touched and verified.

All this was laudable—up to a point. It rid medicine of the superstitions that had encumbered it for the preceding two thousand years and put it on a more rigorous, more scientific footing. But in the process physicians became almost irrationally suspicious of things that could not be weighed, measured or slid under a microscope. Feelings and emotions were too shadowy, too elusive and quite irrelevant to this rational new world of precision medicine. In the early part of this century, however, many of these "imprecise" elements were reintroduced into medicine via the psychoanalytic theories of Sigmund Freud.

Freud's work touched only briefly on the unborn child. Traditional neurological and biological opinion in his day held that a child was not mature enough to feel or experience meaningfully until the second or third year of life, which is why he too thought that personality did not begin developing until then.

But Freud did make one major, if inadvertent, contribution to prenatal psychology. He established beyond all doubt that negative emotions and feelings adversely affect physical health. He called this notion psychosomatic disease. That the diseases he had in mind when he formulated the concept were ulcers and migraine headaches made little difference. Nor does the fact that he was focusing on the negative rather than the positive effects of the mind on health. The central thing was his realization that an emotion could create pain and even physical change in the body. If that was true, some researchers believed, then couldn't an emotion also shape an unborn child's personality?

By the 1940s and '50s, investigators including Igor Caruso and Sepp Schindler of the University of Salzburg, Austria, Lester Sontag and Peter Fodor of the United States, Friedrich Kruse of Germany, Dennis Stott of the University of Glasgow, D. W. Winnicott of the University of London and Gustav Hans Graber of Switzerland were sure maternal emotions did just that to a fetus. But they could not prove it in a laboratory.

As psychiatrists and psychoanalysts, their only tools were their ideas and insights. And if, by the 1950s, they had already flown higher on the wings of those ideas than they had dreamed possible when they began their research, what they still needed was a way of translating those ideas into hard, provable facts that could be verified by their colleagues in the physiological sciences. In short, what they needed was a way of actually studying and testing the unborn child in utero. That was beyond the powers of any machine or device then in existence.

By the mid-sixties, however, medical technology finally caught up with them. And since many of these pioneers lived on to a venerable and vigorous old age (and some are still very much alive), they had the satisfaction of seeing much of their work confirmed by a new generation of researchers. The work of such neurologists as Dominick Purpura of Albert Einstein Medical College in New York City and Maria Z. Salam and Richard D. Adams of Harvard, of such audiologists as Erik Wedenberg of Sweden's Karolinksa Research Institute, and such obstetricians as Antonio J. Ferreria of the Mental Research Institute at Palo Alto and Dr. Albert Liley of the Postgraduate School, National Woman's Hospital, in Aukland, New Zealand, and Dr. Margret Liley, his wife, at last provided what had been so sorely lacking—hard, incontestable physiological evidence that the fetus is a hearing, sensing, feeling being. Indeed, the unborn child who began emerging from the work of these men and women was emotionally, intellectually and physically even more advanced than pioneers like Winnicott and Kruse had imagined.

By his fifth week, for example, studies show that he is already developing an amazingly complex repertoire of reflex actions. By his eighth week, he is not only moving his head, arms and trunk easily, he has already fashioned these movements into a primitive body language—expressing his likes and dislikes with well-placed jerks and kicks. What he especially does not like is being poked at. Push, poke or pinch a mother's stomach and her two-and-a-half-month-old fetus will quickly squirm away (as observed through various techniques).

This concern with comfort may explain why some newborn children are so active at night. In utero, night was a baby's busiest time of day. Lying in bed, his mother was anything but relaxed and restful. With her heartburn, upset stomach and leg cramps, she was forever moving this way, then that way, and invariably there were at least two or three trips to the bathroom. So I do not think it is too surprising that some infants come into the world with an inverted sleep rhythm.

Facial expressions take a little longer than general body movements to master. By his fourth month, the unborn child can frown, squint and grimace. He acquires his basic reflexes at about this time, too. Stroke his eyelids (done experimentally in utero) and he squints instead of jerking his entire body back as he did earlier; stroke his lips and he starts sucking.

Four to eight weeks later, he is as sensitive to touch as any one-year-old. If his scalp is accidentally tickled during a medical examination, he quickly moves his head. He also vehemently dislikes cold water. If it is injected into his mother's stomach, he kicks violently.

Perhaps the most surprising thing about this thoroughly surprising creature is his discriminating tastes. We do not usually think of the fetus as a gourmet. But he is one—of sorts. Add saccharin to his normally bland diet of amniotic fluid and his swallowing rate doubles.

Add a foul-tasting, iodine-like oil called Lipidol and those rates not only drop sharply, but he also grimaces.

Recent studies also show that from the twenty-fourth week on, the unborn child listens all the time. And he has a lot to listen to. The pregnant abdomen and uterus are very noisy places. His mother's stomach rumblings are the loudest sounds he hears. Her voice, his father's voice, and other occasional noises are quieter but still audible to him. The sound that dominates his world, though, is the rhythmic thump of the maternal heartbeat. As long as it is at its regular rhythm, the unborn knows all is well; he feels secure and that sense of security stays with him.

The unconscious memory of the maternal heartbeat in utero appears to be why a baby is comforted by being held to someone's chest or is lulled to sleep by the steady ticking of a clock, and why adults in a busy office are rarely distracted by the rhythmic clacking of typewriters or the steady hum of an air conditioner. Dr. Albert Liley believes it is also why most people, when asked to set a metronome to a rate that satisfies them, usually choose a rate in the range of fifty to ninety beats per minute—roughly the same as the beat of the human heart.

Another expert, Elias Carnetti, thinks the primal memory of one's mother's heartbeat also explains a lot about our musical tastes. All known drum rhythms, he points out, conform to one of two basic patterns—either the rapid tattoo of animal hooves or the measured beat of the human heart. The animal-hoof pattern is easy enough to understand—a distant remnant of man's past as a hunter. Yet it is the heartbeat rhythm that is more widespread in the world—even among the remaining hunting cultures.

Certainly Boris Brott is convinced his musical interests

were awakened in the womb. Many other musicians, among them Arthur Rubinstein and Yehudi Menuhin, make the same claim. Moreover, in an arresting series of new studies audiologist Michele Clements has shown that the unborn child has distinct musical likes and dislikes— and discriminating ones at that.

As I mentioned earlier, Vivaldi is one of the unborn child's favorite composers; Mozart is another. Whenever one of their soaring compositions was put on a phonograph, reports Dr. Clements, fetal heart rates invariably steadied and kicking declined. The music of Brahms and Beethoven, and all forms of rock, on the other hand, drove most fetuses to distraction. They kicked violently when records of these composers were played to their pregnant mothers.

In the 1920s, a German investigator reported an even sharper reaction. Several of his pregnant patients told him they had given up concert-going because their unborn children reacted so stormily to music. Nearly fifty years later, Dr. Liley and his colleagues finally discovered why. The Liley team found that from the twenty-fifth week on, a fetus will literally jump in rhythm to the beat of an orchestra drum, which is certainly not a very restful way to spend an evening.

An unborn child's vision develops more slowly, for obvious reasons: A womb, although not totally dark, is not exactly the ideal place to practice seeing. That doesn't mean a fetus can't see. From the sixteenth week in utero, he is very sensitive to light. He can tell when his mother is sunbathing from the rays that reach him. And while that usually does not disturb him, shining a light directly on his mother's stomach does. He often looks the other way and even if he does not, the light startles him. One researcher produced dramatic fluctuations in fetal heart-beat just by shining a blinking light on a pregnant woman's stomach.

A child's vision is not particularly acute at birth. A new-born has only 20/500 vision, which means he cannot see a tree half a football field away. But neither trees nor football fields have much to do with his life at this point anyway. He can see the objects in *his* world fairly clearly, if they are up close. He can make out most of the features of his mother's face if they are six to twelve inches away. Equally impressive, from as far away as nine feet, he can spot the outline of a finger.

Dr. Liley has a fascinating theory about this. He be-lieves a baby's visual shortcomings may, at least in part, be the after-effects of a habit he picked up in the womb. He argues that if an infant is not much interested in objects more than a foot to a foot and a half away, it is because that distance corresponds to the size of the home he has recently vacated.

The fact that the unborn child has proven abilities to react to his surroundings through his senses shows that he has the basic prerequisites for learning. Personality formation requires something more, however. At an ab-solute minimum, it requires consciousness or awareness. A mother's thoughts and feelings cannot register in a void if they are to be meaningful. Her child has to be acutely aware of what she is thinking and experiencing. Just as essential, he has to be able to read her thoughts and feelings with some subtlety and sophistication. He gets a lot of messages in the womb and he has to be able to tell which are essential and which are not—which mes-sages to act on and which to disregard. Finally, he has to remember what they tell him. If he can't, their content, no matter how critical, will not register for more than a moment or two.

This is a great deal to ask of a very small child, which is why some investigators still vigorously resist the notion that personality begins forming in utero. They argue that the emotional, intellectual and neurological capacities involved in this complex process are far beyond the unborn child's capabilities.

These objections, however, blindly ignore what has been learned in the laboratory. Recent neurological studies not only prove that consciousness, the most important of the three prerequisites, exists in utero, but pinpoint the time it begins. Dr. Dominick Purpura, editor of the highly respected journal *Brain Research*, Professor at Albert Einstein Medical College and head of the study section on the brain of the National Institutes of Health, puts the start of awareness between the twenty-eighth and thirty-second week. By this point, he notes, the brain's neural circuits are just as advanced as a newborn's.* This is critical because messages are relayed across the brain and from the brain to various parts of the body through those circuits. At about the same time, the cerebral cortex matures enough to support consciousness. This is equally important, because the cortex is the highest, most complex part of the brain—the part most distinctly human. It is what we use for thinking, feeling and remembering.

A few weeks later, brain waves become distinct—making it easy to distinguish between the child's sleeping and waking states. Even asleep he is mentally active now. From the thirty-second week on, brain wave tests begin

* This is one of the reasons why the survival rates for premature infants begin rising sharply at the end of the second trimester and thereafter.

picking up periods of REM sleep, which in adults signify the presence of dream states. And while it is impossible to say whether fetal REMs signify the same thing, if the child does dream, I suspect—apart from the difference in experience—his dreams would not be very different from ours. He may dream of moving his hands and feet, for instance, or of hearing noises. He may even be able to tune into the thoughts or dreams of his mother so that her dreams become his dreams.

Another possibility, suggested by three American sleep researchers, Drs. H. P. Roofwarg, J. H. Muzil, and W. C. Dement, is that the REM periods are the fetal brain's equivalent of weight lifting. To develop properly, they argue, it has to exercise itself, and the neurological activity of REM periods is just that—mental exercise.

The first thin slivers of memory track begin streaking across the fetal brain sometime in the third trimester, though exactly when is hard to pinpoint. Some investigators claim a child can remember from the sixth month on; others argue the brain does not acquire powers of recall until at least the eighth month. There is, however, no question that the unborn child remembers or that he retains his memories.

In a recent book, Czechoslovakian psychiatrist Stanislav Grof tells how one man, under medication, portrayed his fetal body very accurately—how large his head was in comparison to his legs and arms—what it felt like to be in warm amniotic fluid, and to be attached to his placenta. Then, while describing his heart sounds and those of his mother, he suddenly broke off midway and announced he could hear muffled noises outside the womb—the laughter and yelling of human voices and the tinny blast of carnival trumpets. Just as suddenly and inexplicably, the man declared he was about to be delivered.

Intrigued by the vividness and detail of this memory, Dr. Grof contacted the patient's mother, who not only confirmed the details of her son's story, but added that it was the excitement of a carnival that precipitated his birth. Still, the woman was surprised by Dr. Grof's query. She had deliberately kept her visit to the carnival secret all these years because she had been warned by her mother that such a thing might happen if she went. How, she wondered, had the doctor learned of her visit?

Whenever I include this story in a lecture, lay people invariably nod their heads knowingly. The notion that an unborn child remembers strikes them as quite natural. The same is true of fetal consciousness: Most people find it a perfectly logical idea, especially women who are or were pregnant. What does provoke puzzled looks and questions from audiences, though, is the claim that an unborn child can sense his mother's thoughts and feelings. How, people ask, can a child decode maternal messages that say "love" and "comfort" when he has absolutely no way of knowing what these feeling states mean?

The first glimmerings of an answer to that question came in 1925, when American biologist and psychologist W. B. Cannon demonstrated that fear and anxiety can be biochemically induced by the injection of a group of chemicals* called catecholamines, which appear naturally in the blood of fearful animals and humans. In Dr. Cannon's experiments, the catecholamines extracted from already frightened animals were injected into a sec-

* This group, which includes epinephrine, norepinephrine and dopamine, act as transmitters within the autonomic nervous system.

ond group of relaxed animals. Within seconds and without provocation, all the calm animals also began acting terrified.

Dr. Cannon subsequently discovered that what produced this unusual effect was the catecholamines' ability to act like a circulating fire alarm system. Once in the bloodstream, they produce all the physiological reactions we associate with fear and anxiety. And whether the blood system happens to be in an animal or unborn child makes little difference. The only distinction in the fetus's case is the source of these substances; they come from his mother when she becomes upset. As soon as they pass the placental barrier, they upset him as well.

Strictly speaking, that makes the unborn child's anxiety and fear largely physiological. The direct, immediate and most measurable impact of maternal hormones is on his body, not his mind. But, in the process, these substances do begin prodding him toward a primitive awareness of himself and of the purely *emotional* side of feeling states. This is a complicated process and we will take a closer look at how it occurs in the next chapter. Suffice it to say here that each wave of maternal hormones jolts him out of the blankness that is his normal state in the womb, and into a kind of receptivity. Something unusual—perhaps unsettling—has happened and because he is human, the fetus begins trying to make sense out of that event. Though he does not frame the question quite this way, what he is really asking himself is "Why?"

Gradually, as his brain and nervous system mature, he will begin finding answers, not just in the physical side of his mother's feeling states, but in the emotional side as well. This process is not as concrete as words make it sound. But, by the sixth or seventh month, an unborn baby is capable of making some fairly subtle discriminations in his mother's attitudes and feelings and, more importantly, starts acting on them.

One of the best demonstrations of this fact I know of is a remarkable series of studies reported by Dr. Dennis Stott in the early 1970s. Given the obvious communication problems, an unborn or newly born child cannot tell us what maternal feelings he sensed in utero or how he reacted to them, but like the rest of us he is subject to the psychosomatic effect. When he is happy, he often blossoms physically; when he is distraught, he just as often becomes sickly and emotionally unstable. And since the chief source of his emotional life in utero is his mother, Dr. Stott reasoned that a child's physical and emotional state at birth and in the years immediately following it would provide a good idea of the kind of maternal messages he received in utero—and how accurately he perceived them.

If he was right, then short-term maternal upsets should not affect a child as deeply as long-term ones. And that is what he found in one of his studies. No ill effects—physical or emotional—were apparent in the offspring of women who had suffered fairly intense but brief stress during pregnancy, such as witnessing a violent dog fight, suffering a scare at work, or having a child of hers run away for a day.

Of course, one might argue that since such frights were short-lived, perhaps the relatively brief exposure to maternal hormones did not harm their children's emotional and physical health. But by that logic all the babies in the study exposed to *intense, long-term* stresses should have been born sickly. They were not, however. In fact, a very fine discrimination among stresses emerged. Dr. Stott's data showed that prolonged upsets that did not directly threaten a woman's emotional security, such as the illness of a close relative, had little or no effect on her unborn child, while long-term *personal* stresses frequently did. More often than not, these were created by tension with a close family member—usually a husband, but in some instances an in-law. According to Dr. Stott, aside from being personal, two other things characterized these stresses. "They tended to be continuous or liable to erupt at any time and they were incapable of resolution." The fact that ten of the fourteen women in the study subjected to these stresses bore children with physical or emotional problems seems, to me, to go beyond anything that can be explained purely in physiological terms. After all, this and the other type of long-term stresses he studied were both intense; hence, equally likely to release large amounts of maternal hormones into the bloodstream.

The only way to make sense of the difference is in terms of perception. In one case, the children were able to sense that while very real, their mother's distress was not threatening to her or them; in the other case, they sensed, accurately, that her distress was a threat.

Unfortunately, one of the things Dr. Stott did not look at in his study is the way the personal-stress mothers felt about their unborn children. If he had, I suspect, he would have found that the intensity of a woman's feeling toward her child can lessen the impact her upsets have on him. Her love is what matters most; and when her child senses that love, it forms a kind of protective shield around him that may decrease or in some cases neutralize, the impact of outside tensions.

It would be hard to imagine a more tumultuous pregnancy than the one a woman I'll call Susan endured. Husbandless—her spouse left her a few weeks after she learned she was expecting—and beset by constant financial problems, Susan had already encountered more than her share of difficulties when, in her sixth month, a pre-cancerous cyst was found on one of her ovaries. Its immediate removal was urged, but when Susan was told that the required surgery would abort her child, she refused. In her mid-thirties, Susan believed this was her last opportunity to have a child and she desperately wanted it. "Nothing else mattered," she told me later. "I would have risked anything to have my baby." On some level, I feel her child sensed that desire. Andrea, as the infant was named, was born healthy and, at this writing, two years later, is a normal, happy, well-adjusted child.

In short, then, while the external stresses a woman faces matter, what matters most is the way she feels about her unborn child. Her thoughts and feelings are the material out of which the unborn child fashions himself. When they are positive and nurturing, the child can, as Andrea did, withstand shocks from almost any quarter. But the fetus cannot be misled either. If he is good at sensing what is on his mother's mind generally, he is even better at sensing her attitude toward him, as a group of ingeniously designed new psychological studies show.

After following two thousand women through pregnancy and birth, Dr. Monika Lukesch, a psychologist at Constantine University in Frankfurt, West Germany, concluded in her study that the mother's attitude had the single greatest effect on how an infant turned out. All her subjects were from the same economic background, all were equally intelligent, and all had the same degree and quality of prenatal care. The only major distinguishing factor was their attitudes toward their unborn children, and that turned out to have a critical effect on their infants. The children of accepting mothers, who looked forward to having a family, were much healthier, emotionally and physically, at birth and afterward, than the offspring of rejecting mothers.

Dr. Gerhard Rottmann of the University of Salzburg, Austria, came to the same conclusion. His study is especially noteworthy because it shows the very fine emotional distinctions the fetus is capable of.

His subjects, 141 women, were placed in one of four emotional categories based on their attitudes toward pregnancy. There were no surprises in the findings from his broadest categories—they duplicated Dr. Lukesch's very closely. The women Dr. Rottmann labeled Ideal Mothers (because psychological testing showed they wanted their unborn children both consciously and unconsciously) had the easiest pregnancies, the most trouble-free births, and the healthiest offspring—physically and emotionally. The women with the negative attitudes, the ones he labeled Catastrophic Mothers, as a group had the most devastating medical problems during pregnancy, and bore the highest rate of premature, low-weight, and emotionally disturbed infants.

The most interesting data, however, came from Dr. Rottmann's two intermediate groups. His Ambivalent Mothers were outwardly quite happy about their pregnancies. Husbands, friends and families all assumed these women could not wait to be mothers. Their unborn children knew differently. Their sensors had picked up the same subconscious ambivalence Dr. Rottmann's psychological tests had. At birth, an unusually large number of them had both behavioral and gastrointestinal problems. The unborn children of Cool Mothers also appeared to be deeply confused about the mixed messages they were picking up. Their mothers had many different reasons for not wanting children—they had careers, they had financial problems, they were not ready to be mothers yet—but Dr. Rottmann's tests showed that subconsciously they desired their pregnancies. On some level their children picked up both messages, and it apparently confused them. At birth, an unusually large number of them were apathetic and lethargic.

What about the father's influence? As I mentioned earlier, all the evidence indicates that the quality of a woman's relationship with her husband or partner—whether she feels happy and secure or, alternatively, ignored and threatened—has a decisive effect on her unborn child. Dr. Lukesch, for example, rates the quality of a woman's relationship to her spouse second only to her attitude toward being a mother in determining infant outcome.

And as we have just seen, Dr. Stott also considers this crucial. He rates a bad marriage or relationship as among the greatest causes of emotional and physical damage in the womb. On the basis of a recent study of over thirteen hundred children and their families, he estimates a woman locked in a stormy marriage runs a 237 percent greater risk of bearing a psychologically or physically damaged child than a woman in a secure, nurturing relationship.

Even such widely recognized dangers as physical illness, smoking and the performance of back-breaking labor during pregnancy pose less of a risk to the unborn child, according to Dr. Stott. And his figures are persuasive. He found unhappy marriages produced children who as babies were five times more fearful and jumpy than the offspring of happy relationships. These youngsters continued to be plagued by problems well into childhood. At four and five, Dr. Stott found them to be undersized, timid and emotionally dependent on their mothers to an inordinate degree. These data are disturbing. But it is also important to remember that a strong, nurturing mother–child bond can protect the fetus against even very traumatic shocks.

Moreover, there are no one-to-one correlations in human psychology. Because a child is the product of an unhappy marriage or the baby of a cool, ambivalent or even catastrophic mother does not necessarily mean he will develop an adult case of schizophrenia, alcoholism, promiscuity or compulsiveness. Nothing about the mind is that neat. But the womb is the child's first world. How he experiences it—as friendly or hostile—does create personality and character *predispositions*. The womb, in a very real sense, establishes the child's expectations. If it has been a warm, loving environment, the child is likely to expect the outside world to be the same. This produces a predisposition toward trust, openness, extroversion and self-confidence. The world will be his oyster, just as the womb has been. If that environment has been hostile, the child will anticipate that his new world will be equally uninviting. He will be predisposed toward suspiciousness, distrust and introversion. Relating to others will be hard, and so will self-assertion. Life will be more difficult for him than for a child who had a good womb experience.

To some extent we can even measure these predispositions. The shyness of those toddlers who had been rated as anxious in utero is one example of prenatal char-

acteristics that were predictive of later behavior; an even
better example is a long-term study on adolescents done
a few years later at the same center, the Fels Research
Institute in Yellow Springs, Ohio. As might be expected,
the investigators did not find a perfect correlation between the subjects' behavior in utero and their behavior
as teenagers. But the relationships that did emerge were
both significant and intriguing.

The measuring stick, in this instance, was heart rate,
which, like activity, is a good indicator of fetal personality. By monitoring it, we can determine how a particular
child reacts to stress and frights (in this instance, their
source was a loud noise made near the mother); and
hence learn something about his personality style. What
makes the Fels findings so significant is not only their
demonstration that, like the rest of us, each unborn baby
reacts to stress in his or her own characteristic way, but
also that reaction tells us something important about a
child's future personality.

Take what I will call the low reactors, the fetuses who,
judging by the continued steadiness of their heartbeat,
were upset very little by the noise. Fifteen years later,
these youngsters were still rarely upset by the unexpected. The researchers found that they remained in
control of their emotions and behavior. In a quite different way, the same correlation was found in the teenagers
who had overreacted (judged by the fluctuations in their
heart rate) to the noise in utero. As a group, they were
still highly emotional. These differences even showed up
in the cognitive or thought styles of the two groups.
When one of what I will call the high-reacting adolescents
was shown a picture by the investigators, he was much
more likely to provide an emotional, creative interpreta-

tion of it, describing not just what was in the picture, but how he thought the people in it felt—whether they were sad or happy, concerned or carefree. The low reactors, on the other hand, tended to offer very concrete descriptions. What they described was what they saw immediately in front of them. There was little or no imagination or flair in their interpretations.*

In the next chapter, we will examine the prenatal forces that help shape character.

* This study shows how careful one has to be when assessing the unborn or newborn's personality. It is dangerous to the future development of the baby to regard him as "good" because he is placid or "bad" because he makes a fuss in utero. Each child has to be allowed to develop his own personality without his parents' prejudging whether he is good or bad.

Chapter Three

The Prenatal Self

The forerunner of the Fels study on adolescents was an unusual paper that appeared late in 1944. Called "War and the Maternal-Fetal Relationship," it grew out of the earlier observations its author, Dr. Lester W. Sontag, had made about the way certain severe maternal anxieties influenced fetal personality development. All these special stresses revolved around threats to the pregnant woman's husband, and it wasn't just that the women subjected to them bore crankier babies. Their infants' problems seemed to Dr. Sontag to be *physically based*. Now that the war had transformed what in peacetime were occasional fears of danger into a daily reality for hundreds of thousands of pregnant women with soldier husbands, he was concerned about the well-being of the children these war mothers were carrying. He suspected those intense maternal anxieties might physically alter a child's emotional regulators in utero and, because of that, many of their babies would behave differently, perhaps more unstably, than infants born in better times.

Today, Dr. Sontag's paper appears remarkably prescient, largely because he correctly foresaw that stresses which increase maternal neurohormonal production—such as the threat to a husband—do heighten a child's *biological susceptibility* to emotional distress. The upsets of such a youngster grow not only out of the psychological consequences of anxiety, but also out of physical ones. Usually one factor is as important as the other in determining the tone and direction of a mind. But in these instances I suspect, as Dr. Sontag did, that the child becomes more emotionally volatile because his body machinery has been significantly altered in utero by an excess flow of his mother's neurohormones. He will continue to grow and change throughout life, but his ability for growth and change will be hindered biologically by his prenatal experiences. Because of his inherent biological limitations, he will sometimes find it harder to function as well as those without these limitations.

Dr. Sontag named this phenomenon *somatopsychics* and defined it as the way "basic physiological processes affect the personality structure, perception and performance of an individual," which makes it the mirror image of psychosomatics. Instead of personality's predisposing the body toward ulcers or hypertension, however, in somatopsychics, the person's body machinery predisposes him toward such psychological disorders as anxiety or depression. Everything we are now learning about the intricate neurohormonal loops* that link mother to unborn child support the notions Dr. Sontag advanced in speculative terms a generation ago.

Physically, mother and child do not share a common

---

* I am referring here to substances such as adrenaline, noradrenaline, serotonin, oxytocin, and so on, which are produced by the body's glands and which by crossing the placenta can affect the unborn.

brain or autonomic nervous system; each has his or her own neurological apparatus and blood-circulation system. So these neurohormonal links are vitally important because they are one of the few ways a mother and her unborn child can carry on an emotional dialogue. Usually the dialogue is initiated by the mother. Her brain, perceiving an action or thought, instantaneously transforms it into an emotion and directs her body to make an appropriate set of responses. The processing itself is done in the cerebral cortex, the brain's outer layer; directly under it, in the hypothalamus, the perception or idea receives an emotional tone and an appropriate set of physical sensations. (This process also works the opposite way. A sensation—for example, pain coming from the arm—will be translated first into an emotion, say fear, in the hypothalamus, and a millisecond later into a thought, "My arm is broken," in the cerebral cortex.)

All the actual sensations we associate with such states as anxiety, depression and excitement start in the hypothalamus, but the actual physical changes emotions produce are created by the two centers it controls—the endocrine system and the autonomic nervous system (ANS). In a pregnant woman who suddenly becomes frightened, the hypothalamus orders the ANS to make the heart beat faster, pupils dilate, palms sweat and blood pressure rise; simultaneously, the endocrine system is signaled to step up neurohormone production. Flooding into the bloodstream, these substances alter the woman's body chemistry and, ultimately, her unborn child's as well. I have used fear as an example, but this process can be triggered by any number of other emotions, which, if intense and ongoing, can alter the unborn child's normal biological rhythms.

One way this happens is by creating an *emotional* predisposition to anxiety. This is more a psychological than a physical process and we will look at how it occurs a bit later. Another more serious way is by creating a *physical* predisposition to anxiety through an alteration in the body's emotional processing centers. Exactly at what point the fetal brain and nervous system are most vulnerable to overflows of stress-related maternal neurohormones we do not know, nor do we yet understand precisely the kinds of changes those neurohormones produce. However, recent evidence indicates that the fetal hypothalamus and its outposts in the body may be particularly vulnerable.

This is significant because, as we have seen, the hypothalamus is the body's emotional regulator. If a child's hypothalamus gets set too high or too low it, or the mechanisms it controls such as the endocrine and autonomic nervous systems, will not operate properly. The evidence supporting the notion of hypothalamic vulnerability takes two forms—direct and indirect. In the latter category falls a report from a team of Columbia University investigators, who measured the effects of famine in utero. What makes their report relevant to our discussion is that it shows how at critical stages in pregnancy an outside factor influences hypothalamic formation. (Among other things, the hypothalamus regulates our food intake.) The Columbia team studied the physical records of Dutch women and their sons who had been subjected to famine.* Severe overweight problems turned out to be common in the group; the degree of

* In late 1944 the Germans placed a severe food embargo on certain sections of Holland, which produced widespread famine. The study was based on the draft-age records of the men whose mothers were pregnant with them during the famine.

susceptibility depended largely on the developmental stage the men (then still unborn babies) were in when famine struck. Suffering severe hunger in the first four or five months of gestation seemed to have the greatest effect; obesity was unusually common among those men whose mothers had been malnourished then. The team concluded that nutritional deprivation in that period affects the setting of the hypothalamic areas regulating food intake and growth.

Direct evidence of the influence of stress on hypothalamic development comes from a new Finnish study. All its subjects had lost their fathers either while in utero or shortly after birth; it was this difference that interested Drs. Matti Huttunen and Pekka Niskanen. Obviously a husband's death puts great stress on a woman which is automatically transmitted to her child. What the researchers wanted to know was when the effect of that stress would be greatest, before or after birth. One look at their subjects' histories gave them an answer: The rates of psychiatric disorders, particularly schizophrenia, were markedly higher among those whose fathers had died before the children were born. To the investigators, this finding seemed to go beyond psychological explanations. To them the before-birth group's unusual incidence of emotional disorders suggested a biological malfunction. Since the hypothalamus is the body's feeling center, they concluded its integration had been adversely affected by maternal distress.

It is important to keep in mind, however, that both these reports measured the effects of *extreme* distress. Famine and the death of a spouse are hardly common experiences for a pregnant woman. Her stresses and anxieties are usually much less severe and, accordingly, so are the effects of these stresses on her child. These more subtle stresses may result in a child who will eat poorly, cry a lot, be cranky, and have loose stools. He is usually diagnosed as "colicky." I suspect such behavior is related to minor stress-induced flaws in the child's hypothalamus and ANS.

Simply put, the hypothalamus and the ANS keep our internal environment working smoothly and efficiently without any conscious effort on our part. If I start running or doing heavy work, this system automatically adjusts my breathing rate; if I walk into a hot room on a cold day, it makes the necessary corrections in my body temperature. It also regulates the body's digestion and elimination processes, so that if for any reason the ANS or its control center, the hypothalamus, malfunctions, gastrointestinal or bowel problems may occur. This is why I think many of the seemingly undiagnosable cases of gastric distress after birth are due to hypothalamic or ANS disorders. Dr. Sontag agrees. Several years ago, he noted in a paper that an irritable or hyperactive ANS could very possibly cause "disturbances of gastrointestinal motility, tone and function." Or as he put it more forcefully in another report: "Because the child's irritability involves the control of his gastrointestinal tract he empties his bowels at unusually frequent intervals, spits up his feedings, and generally makes a nuisance of himself."

While this set of conditions may or may not produce feeding problems, it frequently does produce behavioral ones. A child with an irritable, overcharged ANS tends to be high-strung: restless, fidgety, overactive. In the womb, the precursor of such behavior is excessive movement of the kind exhibited by the shy, anxious toddlers I discussed earlier who had been rated far more active than a comparable group of unborn children. Because of their incessant movement in utero such youngsters are frequently born slightly underweight; and it is worth noting that in reports on poor academic performance in childhood the correlation between low-birth weight and poor reading performance seems to indicate that these children continue to have problems.

Although like most other academic skills reading requires a degree of intelligence, it also takes a certain ability to persist at a task. So it is fair to assume that one of the reasons low-birth-weight babies have trouble reading later is that they are too distractable and restless to sit still long enough to learn how. In other words, their reading problems are a reflection of their behavioral problems. This connection is very prominent in The British National Child Development Study, a large-scale, government-sponsored research project. Not only did the low-birth-weight youngsters in it tend to read more poorly than their schoolmates, the investigators also found they were more likely to be rated as "problems" or "difficult" by teachers. Even more significant, while such factors as sex, order of birth, the mother's smoking or her age at pregnancy correlated with either poor reading performance or behavioral problems, low birth weight was one of the few variables that correlated with both.

At the risk of oversimplification, one could reduce all the findings I have cited into the following formula: Excessive maternal neurohormonal secretion creates an overcharged ANS, which leads to low weight at birth and/or gastric disorders and/or reading difficulties and/or behavioral problems.

On a more hypothetical level, based on some recent

research, one other element could be added: An over-flow of the maternal hormones progesterone and/or estrogen leads to imbalances in the fetal nervous system and brain, which in turn lead to constitutional personality disorders. In this case, however, the personality problems would not be related to hyperactivity, but to the child's sex-role behavior.

Progesterone and estrogen are both present in a pregnant woman's bloodstream. The amount of each depends on an intricate balance of signals between the woman's autonomic and central nervous systems. What controls these signals and, hence, the flow of progesterone and estrogen, is what she is thinking, feeling, doing or saying. In short, like other hormones, these two are ultimately regulated by her emotions. What has suddenly given this long-accepted knowledge an entirely new resonance is a recent study by investigators from the State University of New York (SUNY).

Until the early 1970s, when they were banned for this purpose as unsafe in the United States, estrogen or a combination of estrogen and progesterone was used to prevent miscarriages. Women in danger of aborting received quantities of both hormones much larger than are normally present in their systems. The ban was based on the agents' physical hazards, but the SUNY report was the first to show these drugs carry psychological dangers as well. It found that pregnant women given either or both agents during pregnancy bore children with markedly increased feminine traits. The differences were sharpest in girls. But the hormone-exposed boys were also judged more effeminate, less athletic, and displayed significantly less aggression toward their fathers than the non-exposed boys. Another interesting finding in the male group was the link between type of dosage and behavior: Boys exposed to a combination of estrogen and progesterone had more female traits than those exposed to estrogen alone. But one of the researchers is quick to caution that what the team found "were shifts in temperament, not behavior disorders." Furthermore, women in danger of aborting received quantities of both hormones much larger than is normally present in their systems.

Still, these findings demonstrate what I have been arguing all along: Exposure to excessive amounts of *specific* maternal hormones produces *specific* organically based personality changes in an unborn child. In this instance, hormones came from an outside source; in most others, they come directly from the mother.

Fortunately, physiological imprinting does not necessarily destine a child to a single, narrow path of personality development. The process I have been describing affects his neurological circuitry, and that those circuits are extremely sensitive to malfunctions in the form of underloads, overloads or inconsistencies is undeniable. There is no doubt that core feelings such as love or rejection impinge on the unborn from a very early age. But as his brain matures, primitive sensations and feelings grow into more complex feeling-thought states and later still into pure ideas. Remember, our best evidence indicates the first stirrings of fetal consciousness do not occur until well into the second trimester. A catastrophic stress in the third or fourth month may alter an unborn child's neurological development, but until about the sixth month its effect on him is largely—though not totally—physical. Little cognitive content is attached to stress until then because his brain is not mature enough to translate maternal messages into emotion. Emotion involves not just a sensation but making sense out of the sensation. Rage, for instance, is an inchoate feeling. Only when it receives tone and definition in the higher centers of the brain does it become a complex emotion. To create one, a child must be able to perceive a feeling, make sense out of it, and create an appropriate response. In short, to transform a feeling or a sensation into an emotion requires a perceptive process. That, in turn, involves the ability to do some complex mental calculations at the cerebral cortex level, an ability the child does not attain until his sixth month in utero. Only then, as he gains awareness of himself as a distinct "self" and is able to convert sensations into emotions, does he begin to be shaped increasingly by the *purely emotional* content of his mother's messages.

As his ability to differentiate and distinguish grows, his own emotional development becomes more sophisticated. He is like a computer who is continually being reprogrammed. At first, he can only do very simple emotional equations. As his memory and experience expand, he gradually acquires the ability to make more discriminating and subtle connections. At three months in utero, such complicated maternal messages as ambivalence and coolness largely elude him, though on some primitive level he may feel a sensation of discomfort. By birth, however, the infant is mature enough to be able to respond to maternal feelings with great accuracy and compose physical, emotional and cognitive responses. In the studies we have looked at, for instance, the unhappiness of rejected children is plainly evident in their unusually large number of physical and behavioral problems; the happiness of the accepted babies shows up in the form of their relative tranquillity; and the ambiguity of the infants of cool and ambivalent mothers manifests itself in their halfway responses—as a group they are not quite ill, but not quite well either.

As every high school biology student knows, living things progress from simplicity to complexity. Physically, just as an unborn child develops in nine months from a tiny undifferentiated speck of protoplasm into a highly defined creature with a complex brain, nervous system, and body, emotionally he grows from an insensate being into one who can register and process very intricate and perplexing feelings and emotions.

Another term for this development is *ego formation*. Ego is the sum of what we as individuals think and feel about ourselves; our strengths, drives, desires, vulnerabilities and insecurities all go into shaping the distinct "I" that is each of us. As soon as a child is capable of remembering and feeling—in other words, of being marked by experience—his ego is forming.

As I have pointed out, Freud believed ego began operating between a child's second and fourth year, not an unreasonable hypothesis given the evidence available to him at the time. We now know more about the first months of life—physically, psychologically and neurologically—than Freud could even have guessed. Yet, inexplicably, very little of this knowledge has seeped into the current theories on ego, so it will probably be a decade or two before ego formation in utero becomes part of accepted psychiatric thinking. The mechanics of ego formation, however, have largely been worked out; all we have to do now is learn to apply them to the prenatal period.

Because the fetus is mature enough by the second trimester, I believe the unborn's ego begins to function sometime in that period. His nervous system is now capable of transmitting sensations to his higher brain centers. The value of these largely physiological messages is that they foster the neurological development required for more complicated tasks later. Say, for instance, that a woman's particularly hectic day has tired her unborn child. That tiredness creates a primitive feeling—discomfort—which brings the unborn baby's nervous system into play; his attempt to make sense of that feeling involves his brain. After enough of these episodes, his perceptual centers become advanced enough to process more complex and subtle maternal messages. (Like the rest of us, the unborn gets better with practice.)

To show how this process begins in utero, let me trace the contribution of one common maternal emotion—anxiety—to ego development. Anxiety, within limits, is beneficial to the fetus. It disturbs his sense of oneness with his surroundings and makes him aware of his own separateness and distinctness. It also pushes him into action. Being excited, upset or confused by noisy messages is an uncomfortable experience, so he kicks, he squirms, he gradually begins devising ways of getting out of the way of anxiety—in short, he starts erecting a set of primitive defense mechanisms. In the process, his experience of anxiety and what to do about it slowly becomes more sophisticated. What began as a blunt, displeasing feeling he could only distinguish as uncomfortable, over the months grows into something quite different. It becomes an emotion, acquires a source (his mother), prompts his thoughts about that source's intentions toward him, forces him to conjure up ways of dealing with those intentions, and creates a string of memories that can be referred to later.

The foundations of anger are laid in much the same way, though its roots differ. We know a newborn has a special "mad" cry, and one of the things that produces it is restraining his movement. Hold his arm or leg and he screams furiously. Almost certainly, blocking his behavior has the same effect before birth as it does afterward. If his mother happens to sit or lie in an uncomfortable position, he becomes annoyed. Unpleasant sounds—such as his father's yelling—also make him react this way. As with anxiety, however, anger in small doses actually benefits fetal development since it hastens the development of rudimentary intellectual connections. In the case of restraint, for example, the child learns something about cause and effect—the way his mother sits or lies causes cramps and, hence, angers him—and that is a precursor of human thought.

Some forms of depression can also originate in utero. Usually, these are produced by a major loss. For whatever reason—illness or a distraction—a mother withdraws her love and support from her unborn child; that loss plunges him into a depression. You can see the aftereffects of this in an apathetic newborn or a distracted sixteen-year-old; for, like other emotional patterns set in utero, depression may plague a child for the rest of his life. This is why treating infant depressions has recently become one of psychiatry's chief priorities.

Moreover, such feelings as depression, anger and anxiety contribute to the growth of consciousness and self-awareness. Dutch psychiatrist Lietaert Peerbolte's elegant formulation of this process is "seeing is the interruption of vision," and that is not only a beguiling but also a particularly apt metaphor since the child's normal state in the womb is, like vision, blank and unfocused. Seeing, in Peerbolte's formulation, is what happens when an outside intrusion suddenly disrupts this fetal serenity. In these moments, the child is like a walker who has been gazing at a landscape when his eyes unexpectedly fall on a beautiful church steeple in the distance. Just as the sight of the steeple suddenly attracts the walker's attention, produces an unusual feeling, awe, in him which leaves a memory, so an outside intrusion forces the child out of his blankness, concentrates his attention, elicits an emotional response and, as all unusual or exceptional incidents do, produces a memory trace. When the number of these moments and memories reaches a certain critical level, Dr. Peerbolte believes as I do that they coalesce into self-awareness in much the same way water particles turn into ice crystals when the temperature falls below freezing.

This theory, like all good theories, makes sense of many seemingly disparate facts in ego formation. Dr. Peerbolte's construction not only explains how the "I" forms in utero but the role a mother's emotions play in shaping that "I." If loving, nurturing mothers bear more self-confident, secure children, it is because the self-aware "I" of each infant is carved out of warmth and love. Similarly, if unhappy, depressed or ambivalent mothers bear a higher rate of neurotic children, it is because their offsprings' egos were molded in moments of dread and anguish. Not surprisingly, without redirection, such children often grow into suspicious, anxious and emotionally fragile adults.

Dr. Paul Bick, a West German physician and pioneer in the use of hypnotherapy, recently treated a man who fit that description perfectly. The man complained of severe anxiety attacks accompanied by hot flushes. To uncover their source, Dr. Bick put the patient into a trance. Slowly moving back across the months he had spent in the womb, the man recalled particular incidents, always describing them in a calm, level voice until he reached his seventh month. Then, suddenly his voice tightened and he began to panic. Clearly, he had arrived at the experience that had become the prototype for his problem. He felt terribly hot and afraid. What caused this? The patient's mother supplied the answer a few weeks later: During a long and anguished conversation, she confessed she had attempted to abort him in her seventh month of pregnancy by taking hot baths.

What we know about fetal behavior in utero also fits Dr. Peerbolte's formulation. If, in the months prior to birth, the child's behavior grows increasingly more sophisticated and directed, it is because a conscious "I" is now guiding it, supported by and drawing from a growing memory bank. On some level all emotional conflicts grow out of memories, whether the recollections are conscious ones or, as is more often the case, unconscious. Dr. Bick's patient, for instance, did not remember the source of his anxiety attacks, but that did not make the terror that sprung from that source any less real—more than two decades later his behavior was still being guided by a submerged but potent prenatal memory. All of us have lost memories that from their hiding place—the unconscious—can exert a powerful influence over our lives.

A few years ago, Canadian neurosurgeon Wilder Penfield demonstrated this in a series of daring clinical experiments. By applying a special electrical prober to the surface of the brain, Dr. Penfield was actually able to make a person emotionally re-experience a situation or event he or she had long forgotten.* Each patient, Dr. Penfield wrote in his report on the experiments, "does not just remember exact photographic or phonographic reproductions of past scenes and events . . . he feels again the emotions which the situation actually produced in him . . . what [he] saw and heard and felt and understood." This is why long-forgotten slights, defeats and conflicts continue to pull at us. Even our most deeply buried memories have emotional resonances, which influence us in perplexing and often troubling ways.

A story I heard from a colleague, Dr. Gary Maier, illustrates this point. A gentle, insecure patient of his, whom I'll call Fred, had a startling recollection one day under medication. In the middle of a session, he suddenly began describing an enclosed room. He said he had been there for a while and was enjoying himself, but now the mood in the room was changing; people were crowding around him, pointing their fingers accusingly at him. He felt angry and frightened, and he didn't know what to do. Neither doctor nor patient understood the meaning of this eerie story. But Fred's curiosity was aroused by it, so a few days later, he mentioned it to his mother. The mystery was solved: Fred's tale was a slightly—but only slightly—distorted prenatal memory. The scene he described had, in fact, happened to his mother when she was carrying him, and the incident was every bit as frightening and humiliating as Fred's experience of it. She was in a roomful of people at a party when several of her friends learned she was illegitimately pregnant.

---

* Because the brain has no pain fibers, Dr. Penfield was able to operate on conscious patients. In the course of surgery, he would stimulate different parts of the brain with an electrical probe.

Although they said nothing, their unspoken criticism hurt her deeply.

By now it should be clear that we know a good deal about the way events and situations shape our personalities. We know that love and caring are essential to the development of a strong "I," while maternal anxiety and stress appear to threaten it on nearly every level. What we still don't know enough about, however, is which specific prenatal events produce specific personality traits.

The few—largely government sponsored—studies that have attempted to measure the long-term effects of prenatal and birth experiences on children's later academic performance have not gone far enough to be of much help either.

These reports tell us very little, really, about why some children do better in school than others or about the events or situations that produce the emotionally stable, secure "self" so essential to a good performance in school and in life. Nor, most crucially, do they tell us what part a child's prenatal and birth histories play in shaping or undermining the stability of that "self."

One day, perhaps, we will get that kind of data. In the meantime, we can learn something from the results of a pilot project I conducted in 1979. Though my work was modest in scope and done on a highly select population —people undergoing depth-oriented psychotherapy—I believe the results represent significant predictors of future behavior.

I structured the study around two basic categories: prenatal events and birth experiences (which will be examined separately in a later chapter). Then, since I felt it would make interpretation easier, I subdivided those broad categories into two smaller ones: objective events and subjective feelings. That made it possible to distinguish between what people thought influenced them and what really did influence them.

As might be expected of any group in psychotherapy, my subjects tended to have highly charged prenatal and birth histories: 66 percent described their mothers as being under a lot of stress during pregnancy; 47 percent said she was seriously unhappy. Still, 55 percent said their mothers had been looking forward to motherhood, as opposed to 45 percent who reported a negative attitude. The ratios for fathers were only slightly narrower: 51 percent said their fathers wanted a child, 49 percent, that they had not. Twice as many fathers preferred a boy to a girl. Since most of the subjects were born during the heyday of bottle feeding in the 1940s and '50s, very few had been breastfed: Only 16 percent reported having been put to their mother's breast after birth.

The results from the subjective section were more enlightening. Peacefulness was the most commonly reported womb feeling (43 percent), but it was followed very closely by anxiety (41 percent). There was a high incidence of traumatic birth memories: Over 60 percent of the subjects said they had remembered feeling suffocated during birth, and well over 40 percent reported having either head, neck or shoulder pain. Because of the unusual nature of the study group I think these figures may be slightly distorted; a more normal group of individuals would probably have a somewhat lower incidence of damaging prenatal and birth memories. But one of the advantages of studying a therapy group is the magnification effect, which makes correlations sharper and easier to observe. For example, 75 percent of the subjects described themselves as introverts and 65 percent said they presently felt angry, depressed or anxious.

This last set of numbers brings us to the real heart of the study—an analysis of the prenatal experiences that were at the root of their discontent. By far, the most critical factor was maternal attitude. The study data indicated a subject stood a much better chance of growing into an emotionally stable adult if his mother looked forward to his birth. A strong correlation also emerged between maternal disposition toward pregnancy and adult sexual functioning. Generally, the more positive a mother feels about childbearing, the more likely her son or daughter will grow to adulthood with a healthy, mature sexual attitude.

It should be pointed out, however, that the best combination for personality development was a positive pregnancy attitude *and* getting a child of the desired sex. In both men and women that combination produced less depression, less irrational anger and better sexual adjustment. It says a great deal about our society that a man whose mother had wanted a girl only to get a boy suffered fewer appreciable long-term effects than a woman born to a mother who had wanted a boy.

Like many other reports, mine also uncovered a strong correlation between maternal smoking and neurotic behavior, which isn't surprising, since, as we saw in the first chapter, smoking may predispose an unborn child to severe anxiety. The same negative correlation turns up with drinking, and though the physical effect of alcohol on the fetus is far more devastating than that of cigarettes, I believe, again, that what is being measured here is a psychological variable. The woman drinks more because she is disturbed and it is her negative feelings that really harm her child.

Unquestionably, one of the most fascinating correlations to emerge from my study was the link between subjective womb feelings and adult sexual behavior. We found that people who recalled being terrified in utero were markedly more unsure of themselves sexually and also more prone to sexual problems, while those who remembered the womb as a good and peaceful place were sexually better adjusted.

I think this is because a person's sexual tastes are an expression of how he learned to feel about himself in utero. If this theory is correct it means that what the study really measured here was not sexual attitudes so much as the things that shape them. Presumably a person who defines himself as outgoing and well balanced generally will define himself that way sexually, while someone whose self-definition is colored by anger and resentment will bring those traits to his sex life.

If I seem to dwell excessively on the negative side of a woman's thoughts and feelings in this chapter, it is only because negative emotions have been studied far more exhaustively than such positive ones as nurturing. I am afraid we physicians sometimes manifest an overly energetic interest in the morbid and pathological at the expense of the healthy and life-sustaining. A change of emphasis is now in order. My study uncovered several aspects of maternal feeling—for example, wanting a child and getting the boy or girl desired—which produce *positive* psychological benefits. Certainly, there are many, many more such traits and in the next chapter we will see how the unborn child benefits from them.

Chapter Four

Intrauterine Bonding

Several years ago, I came across a report by a Swiss pediatrician named Stirnimann that was remarkable. The more so because his subject—the sleeping patterns of newborns—wasn't new; medical libraries are full of reports on neonate sleeping habits. But Dr. Stirnimann had added an ingenious twist to his study. Instead of beginning at birth and looking for explanations as other investigators had, he had moved back one step—to the womb.

That imaginative shift produced a dramatic difference. His results showed there is a simple reason why newborns sleep when they do, and it has nothing to do with feeding schedules, nursery routines or anything else that happens after birth. A child's sleeping patterns are set months before, in utero, by his mother. In his study, Dr. Stirnimann demonstrated this fact with exemplary simplicity. He chose two groups of pregnant women with different sleeping habits—early risers and late-nighters —then studied their infants' sleeping schedules after birth. As he suspected, all the early risers bore early-rising babies; all the late-to-bed mothers had late-to-bed children.

This near-perfect example of bonding before birth—and that's the only phrase that accurately describes it—is what excited me so much about the study. By simply taking that one step backward, Dr. Stirnimann was able to show that unborn children can adjust their rhythms to their mothers' with as much precision as newborn babies can.

Of course, we already know how crucial bonding is for newborns. Babies who synchronize with their mothers often benefit. Still, this synchronizing is complex; and the fact that so many mothers and babies are able to carry it out flawlessly on the first try has always intrigued me.

Recent evidence suggests that some of the mother's responses are biologically regulated. But even with that advantage, how could a mother and unborn child perform such an elaborate and perfectly timed dance without the benefit of rehearsal beforehand?

Dr. Stirnimann's study showed that months before birth, mother and child were already beginning to mesh their rhythms and responses to each other. This pointed squarely to one conclusion: Bonding after birth, which had always been studied as a singular and isolated phenomenon, was actually the continuation of a bonding process that began long before, in the womb.

The eminent Harvard pediatrician T. Berry Brazelton had suggested as much previously. Speaking at a symposium on bonding, he had hypothesized that mothers and children who meshed immediately at birth might be drawing on a communications system established earlier in pregnancy. This theory was largely borne out a few years later by a discovery made by biologists at the City University of New York. Although their findings came from animal, not human research, the intrauterine communication system they discovered between mother hen and unborn chick worked pretty much the way Dr. Brazelton suggested such a system would operate in people. It was built around a series of elaborate and quite specific cues,* and it aided in post-birth adaptation just as he thought it would. The investigators found that chicks who had been hatched by their mothers were much more responsive to their mothers' calls and made an easier adjustment to their new environment than those who had been incubated in a mechanical brooder.

It is fair to assume that if such a system operates in an animal fairly far down the evolutionary scale, a similar though much more advanced system operates in us. Several new human studies support this conclusion. In fact, what emerges from all these new reports is a picture of a human intrauterine bonding system at least as complex, graded and subtle as the bonding that occurs after birth. Indeed, they are part of the same vital continuum: What happens after birth is an elaboration of, and depends on, what happened prior to it.

This realization explains the source of the newborn's surprisingly accomplished post-birth performance. His ability to respond to his mother's hugs, stroking, looks and other cues is based on his long acquaintance with her prior to birth. After all, sensing his mother's body and eye language is not very challenging to a creature who

---

* Unborn chicks were found to have special distress and pleasure calls; hens a specific response to each. For instance, a distress call would produce a reassuring sound or movement in the mother that instantly quieted the frightened chick.

has honed his cue-reading skills in utero on the far more difficult task of learning to respond to her mind. The reports of Drs. Lukesch and Rottmann have demonstrated his awesome powers in this area. An even more impressive example of maternal–unborn communication came in a paper delivered by a highly respected Austrian obstetrician named Emil Reinold at a recent meeting of the International Society of Prenatal Psychology. While its subject was fetal reaction to maternal emotion, it also demonstrated how the unborn becomes an active participant in intrauterine bonding.

Like Dr. Stirnimann's report, this one was disarmingly simple in design. Pregnant women were asked to lie prone for twenty to thirty minutes on a table under an ultrasound machine. What Dr. Reinold deliberately did not tell them was that when a woman lies like this, her child eventually quiets down and lies still too. As each child relaxed, his mother was only told that the ultrasound screen showed her baby wasn't moving. The terror that information produced was expected and deliberate. Dr. Reinold wanted to see how quickly a mother's fear registered on her child and how he reacted when it did. In every case, the response was swift: Seconds after each woman learned her child was lying motionless, the image on the ultrasound screen began stirring. None of the babies were in any imminent danger, but as soon as they sensed their mothers' distress, they began kicking mightily.

Very likely, part of their reaction was due to the rise in maternal adrenaline levels produced by Dr. Reinold's frightening announcement, but only part. On another level, these children were also reacting sympathetically to their mothers' distress.

A child whom I'll call Kristina provides an even more

graphic example of intrauterine bonding. I learned about her from Dr. Peter Fedor-Freybergh, a boyhood friend of mine who is now a professor of obstetrics and gynecology at the University of Uppsala in Sweden and one of Europe's leading obstetricians.

Everything had begun fine, Peter said. At birth, Kristina was robust and healthy. Then something strange happened. Bonding babies invariably move toward the maternal breast, but inexplicably, Kristina didn't. Each time her mother's breast was offered, she turned her head away. At first, Peter thought she might be ill, but when Kristina devoured a bottle of formula milk in the nursery later, he decided her reaction was a temporary aberration. It wasn't. The next day, when Kristina was brought to her mother's room, she refused her breast again; the same thing happened for several days thereafter.

Concerned, but also curious, Peter devised a clever experiment. He told another patient of his about Kristina's baffling behavior and that woman agreed to try breastfeeding the child. When a sleepy Kristina was placed in her arms by a nurse, instead of spurning the woman's breast as she had her mother's, Kristina grasped it and began sucking for all she was worth. Surprised by her reaction, Peter visited with Kristina's mother the next day and told her what had happened. "Why do you suppose the child reacted that way?" he asked. The woman said she didn't know. "Was there an illness during her pregnancy, perhaps?" he suggested. "No, none," she replied. Peter then asked, point-blank, "Well, did you want to get pregnant then?" The woman looked up at him and said, "No, I didn't, I wanted an abortion. My husband wanted the child. That's why I had her."

That was news to Peter but, obviously, not to Kristina.

She had been painfully aware of her mother's rejection for a long time. She refused to bond with her mother after birth because her mother had refused to bond with her before it. Kristina had been shut out emotionally in the womb and now, though barely four days old, she was determined to protect herself from her mother in any way she could.

In time, if Kristina's mother changes her attitude she will probably be able to win her affection back. But that affection would already have been established if they bonded before Kristina was born.

They may differ in time and circumstances, but the effects of intra- and extrauterine bonding are nearly always the same. Just as the emotional patterns established immediately after birth are long-term and often decisive in shaping the mother–child relationship, so too are those before birth. The two also share specific time frames—the best period for extrauterine bonding being the hours and days immediately after birth; for intrauterine bonding, the last three months of pregnancy and especially the last two, by which time the child is mature enough physically and intellectually to send and receive fairly sophisticated messages.

The mother's role in both is also similar. She sets the pace, provides the cues and molds her child's responses. But only if he decides her requests make sense to him. Even a three- or four-month-old unborn baby will not follow his mother lemming-like. If her moves are confusing, contradictory, careless or hostile, he may ignore or become confused by them.

In short, intrauterine bonding does not happen automatically: Love for the child and understanding of one's own feelings are needed to make it work. When these are

present, they can more than offset the emotional disturbances we are all prone to in our daily lives.

The unborn child is an amazingly resilient being who
can make even a little maternal emotion stretch a long
way if he has to. But he cannot bond alone. If his mother
shuts down emotionally, he is at a loss. That is why major
psychotic illnesses such as schizophrenia usually make
bonding impossible—and also one reason why the offspring of schizophrenic mothers have such a high rate of
emotional and physical problems.

An external tragedy* sometimes has the same effect
on an otherwise normal, healthy woman. In her case, as
in the schizophrenic's, bonding can be seriously weak-
ened or frayed—for much the same reason. Her child
lacks a feeling person to whom he can attach himself. His
mother becomes absorbed in herself and has no emotional resources left for the baby.

Two cases in point in the form of real-life tragedies
were described several years ago by Dr. Sontag. Because
he had been studying both women on an ongoing basis
since early in their pregnancies, Dr. Sontag had a unique
vantage point: He was able to measure the immediate
effect of the tragedy on each unborn and then, after
birth, its long-term effects.

"In one instance," he wrote, "a young woman carrying
her first baby, which we had been studying weekly . . . in
terms of activity and heart rate, took refuge at our institute one evening because her husband had just suffered
a psychotic breakdown and was threatening to kill her.

---

* Such major catastrophes as the loss of her home or the death of a loved one
can deplete a pregnant woman's emotional reserves to such an extent that she
is unable to extend herself emotionally to her unborn child. This will naturally
be felt by her baby.

She felt terrified and alone and didn't know where to turn for help. She came to our institute and we gave her a bed and room for the night. When she complained a few minutes later that the kicking of the fetus was so violent as to be painful, we recorded the child's activity level. It was tenfold what it had been in the weekly sessions.

"Another case came to our attention when a woman we had been studying lost her husband in an automobile accident. Again, the violent activity and frequency of fetal movement increased by a factor of ten."

Superficially, these babies' reactions look like those of the children who reacted sympathetically to their mothers' distress in Dr. Reinold's study, but the resemblance is misleading. What Dr. Sontag measured was not a sympathetic reaction but the wholesale terror of a child whose system was being flooded by his mother's anxiety-provoking hormones. The fact that each baby was born underweight, and was colicky, cranky, irritable and cried a lot, confirms that each had undergone a serious trauma, since these problems almost invariably are associated with major emotional upheavals in utero. If Dr. Sontag had included more follow-up data on these infants in his report, though, I suspect it would have shown that their post-birth disturbances had less to do with the physical effects of those hormones than with the way the tragedies changed their mothers' emotional attitudes toward them, because what often endangers an unborn child most is not his mother's immediate physical-hormonal reaction to an event, but her long-term emotional one. If she becomes so distracted by her own pain and loss that she withdraws into herself, very likely her child will suffer terribly. But if she keeps the channels between herself and the child open and flowing with reassuring messages, he can continue to thrive. As I said earlier, a strong intrauterine bond is a child's ultimate protection against the outside world's dangers and uncertainties, and as we have seen, its effects are not limited to the uterine period. To a large extent this bond also determines the future of the mother–child relationship. For both, all that comes afterward hinges on what happens now, which is why it is so critical that mother and child remain attuned to each other.

This occurs through three separate communications channels. With one or two exceptions, these systems appear to be equally capable of carrying messages from baby to mother or from mother to baby. The first, physiological, is the only one of the three that is in a sense inevitable; even a rejecting mother communicates with her child biologically, if in no other way than to provide him with nutrients. But as we shall see, how mother and child employ this particular route also makes a critical difference.

The second avenue, behavioral, is the best understood and easiest to observe of the three. For instance, hundreds of studies have documented that unborn babies kick when they are uncomfortable, scared, anxious or confused. Lately, investigators have discovered that a mother communicates behaviorally with her unborn child in certain distinct ways, too. One of the most common of these is by rubbing the stomach—this gesture of reassurance has been found to be nearly universal among pregnant women.

The third route, in many ways the hardest to define, I call sympathetic communication. It almost certainly contains elements of the first two, but it is broader and deeper. Love is a good example. How does a six-month-old fetus know he is loved? Because his mother strokes her stomach, eats sensibly and acts on his behavioral messages? These are all part of the answer, but not all of it.

The crying rate of newborns provides another example of sympathetic communication. Why is it that even very young Chinese babies cry less than American ones? The fact that they do says a great deal about the culture each infant is born into, but how does a three-week-old —or even a three-month-old—infant know enough to behave the way his culture expects him to? The answer, I believe, is again sympathetic communication. Yet another example of it can be found in rural areas of Africa where women carry their newborns, sacklike, on their backs or slung on their sides. Held either way, a baby can easily soil his mother's clothes with his bowel and bladder eliminations. But this almost never happens to an African mother. Somehow she is able to sense his urges in enough time to swing him off her back and hold him away from her before he eliminates. This form of intuitive knowledge is hardly considered unusual. In fact, an African woman soiled by her child after his seventh day of life is loudly and widely branded a poor mother.

People in rural societies nearly always are more intuitive than urban dwellers, probably because they are more willing to trust their senses. Rationalization and mechanization of the kind that has spread across Europe and America over the past few centuries seems to destroy that trust. Nature's enigmas make us uncomfortable. If we cannot explain something, we prefer to ignore it. This does not mean that our past or the African present represents a kind of obstetrical Utopia. In both, infant mortality rates were and are too high. The ideal would be a blend of the extraordinary maternal sensitivity common in those rural societies and our own high standards of medical care. With bonding, we have already taken one important step in that direction. With intrauterine bonding, we can take the next.

More research will be needed, as well as new and more sensitive attitudes. Obstetricians, pediatricians, psychiatrists, nurses, midwives, hospital administrators—everyone who comes into contact with the pregnant woman can learn to be more supportive, more nurturing and less ready to apply medical solutions to what are really emotional problems. But, ultimately, the success or failure of bonding before birth, like bonding after it, lies with the woman herself. She has to start paying closer attention to the messages she sends her child and those he sends her. That requires knowledge: knowledge of the routes along which they communicate and knowledge of the messages that travel along these routes. It also requires a willingness to listen: Her child has a great deal to say and he should be listened to.

BEHAVIORAL COMMUNICATION

Child

Kicking is the unborn's most easily measured form of communication, and any number of things may provoke it, from fear to a well-meaning but noisy father, as audiologist Michele Clements discovered one day when the skeptical husband of one of her patients unexpectedly appeared in her laboratory. The man's wife had told him about Dr. Clements' work, but he found it hard to believe that his child could hear. Seeing that her data were not going to convince him, Dr. Clements suggested a practical demonstration. She told him to press his head against his wife's abdomen and yell. What followed was a textbook-perfect example of behavioral communication (and also an unambiguous display of fetal temper). As the man yelled, a small volcano of skin suddenly erupted on his wife's abdomen. Highly annoyed, the child had registered his protest at this noisy intrusion with a furious kick to his mother's midsection.

Another sound that provokes an emphatic fetal response is the hard, throbbing beat of rock music. As I have said before, unborn children do not like it. One of Dr. Clements' patients discovered this when she was driven from a rock concert by the violent kicking of her baby. Even more distressing to fetal ears are the loud, angry voices of fighting parents. Often this prompts kicking by the unborn.

Kicking can also be a sign of fetal distress. A young woman whom I will call Diane is convinced that that is what set off the furious kicking of her baby. For the first seven months of pregnancy he had been relatively quiet; the little kicking he did was normal for a child of his age. Then, one afternoon in the middle of her twenty-eighth week, Diane felt a sharp jab in her abdomen. At first she dismissed it. She had been out shopping that afternoon and thought all the running around might have tired her child. But by evening his kicking had grown so intense it was impossible to ignore. Worried, Diane called her obstetrician and made an appointment for the next day.

His diagnosis of placenta previa* the following morn-

---

* A placenta that has come to lie very low in the uterus and is in danger of becoming detached, thus endangering the life of the unborn child.

ing may have been coincidental, of course, though Diane thinks her child's subsequent behavior makes that unlikely. She is convinced he was kicking to signal his distress, because after the diagnosis was made and proper treatment was instituted he quieted down again and remained calm until birth.

Maternal emotions such as anger, anxiety and fear will also prompt furious kicking. A good example of this are those tragic babies Dr. Sontag described who suffered because of their mothers' serious stress. In these instances what causes the baby to kick is usually a combination of "outside" and "inside" events. The mother's anxiety-provoking hormones are flooding his system, making him worried and fearful. Her behavior and her emotions are also affecting him. Almost anything that upsets her also upsets him, and nearly as quickly. New studies show that within a fraction of a second after fear has set his mother's heart racing, his begins pounding at double his normal rate.

Mother

Many of the ways a woman communicates behaviorally with her child are so subtle and seemingly ordinary that it is easy to overlook their effect on intrauterine bonding. For example, a large number of couples move into a new home during pregnancy. In one recent study, 79 percent of the women interviewed said they were planning to change their residences because of the new addition to the family. Of course, it is not moving as such that is the problem, but rather the disruptions and the anxiety that accompany moving that is the culprit. In a landmark report, Dr. R. L. Cohen showed that the stress triggered by moving to a new area during pregnancy may delay bond formation between mother and child after birth. Fortunately, if the mother knows about such correlations, she can compensate for them by getting extra rest and emotional support as well as doing some "explaining" to her baby.

Some of Dr. Cohen's other findings were also related to bonding—though less directly. A woman who is occasionally preoccupied by the way she looks; or who thinks she looks ugly; or whose mood changes are abrupt; or who cannot seem to make preparations for her child's birth, is not acting in a way that will actively or directly damage her baby. But Dr. Cohen believes that when all of these behaviors are present throughout the pregnancy they can be indicative of a subconscious rejection of motherhood with consequent impact on bonding.

Another subtle behavioral change that a mother may unwittingly convey to her child is unhappiness about leaving her job during pregnancy. According to one study, as many as 75 percent of working women either quit their jobs or take a leave of absence during pregnancy. In itself, this is neither good nor bad. Some women prefer to keep working well into their last trimester; others cannot wait to leave their jobs. Either choice is fine. The danger arises when the sudden loss of financial and psychological independence created by leaving work causes resentment, anger or dissatisfaction. A child cannot bond with a mother who is seething with anxiety or frustration, no matter how hard he tries.

Even the way a woman moves and paces herself throughout the day becomes a form of behavioral communication. Rushing about madly to get chores and errands done, she moves at a different rhythm than when she is out on a long, unhurried stroll—and her child senses the difference, just as a month or two later he senses when she is pushing him along in a carriage and when she is bouncing him up and down on her knee. In moderation, such activity is perfectly harmless. The unborn child is remarkably resilient, but it is dangerous to push him to the limits of his endurance through excessive, continual stimulation.

SYMPATHETIC COMMUNICATION

Child

Dreams are not random or arbitrary events. They happen for a reason, and in the case of a pregnant woman, I think many dreams express her unconscious conflicts about the child. Expectant mothers who have anxiety-ridden dreams tend to have shorter labors and smoother births. Recent evidence indicates that dreams are one of the common and beneficial ways pregnant women deal with their anxieties. I also know there are dozens of documented cases in the medical literature of pregnant women's dreams that have turned into reality. From conversations with colleagues, I suspect that hundreds, perhaps thousands of other such "coincidences" go unreported because the dreamer or her doctor is afraid of being labelled superstitious or unscientific. These prenatal dreams conform to what we know about the laws of dreaming. There is always an underlying logic to them. No matter how different each dream may be in content, the same patterns and themes appear again and again. The dreamer finds herself confronting her child, almost always in an alarming or urgent situation.

The night before one of my patients had a spontaneous abortion, she shouted herself awake several times, yelling "I want out, let me out." She is convinced that was her child speaking through her. A colleague told me about the dream of a patient of his, which, though quite different in every respect, had the same underlying theme—a child trying frantically to convey a message. At the beginning of her third trimester, his patient dreamed she was about to go into labor. Her pregnancy had been uncomplicated physically and emotionally and nothing in either her medical or psychological history indicated a risk of prematurity. But the dream disturbed her. Convinced that it had a meaning, she began to make preparations for birth "just in case." Two weeks later she delivered.

At this point, one can only speculate about the mechanisms involved in these prenatal dreams. I believe that they are a kind of extrasensory communication from the child. Lately this phenomenon has received a good deal of serious scientific attention. At Duke University a special extrasensory research unit has been studying it for several decades, and the American Association for the Advancement of Science, one of the most august and respected scientific bodies in the world, has been sufficiently impressed with the potential importance of extrasensory forms of communication to sponsor several research projects. It will be interesting to see what sort of results they eventually come up with.

Mother

What we know about sympathetic communication from mother to child tends to bear out the theory of extrasensory communication in the young. Nearly every emotion a woman has seems to contain a sympathetic dimension. Even feelings with a clear biological basis, such as fear and anxiety, affect a child in ways that go beyond anything we know about physiology. This is doubly true of emotions that lack any apparent biological anchor, like love or acceptance. Nothing we know about the human body can explain why these feelings affect the unborn child. Yet study after study shows that happy, content women are far more likely to have bright, outgoing infants.

A highly complex, subtle emotion such as ambivalence provides an even better example. As we have seen, ambivalence can have a harmful effect on an unborn. Yet, there is almost certainly no physiological state connected with it. The emotion is often so muted, the woman herself isn't even aware of it. I think the only logical explanation for these findings is what I have called "sympathetic communication." Evidently the child's emotional radar is so sharp that even the slightest tremors of maternal emotion register with him.

In its own grim way, the data on spontaneous abortion and its incidence also tells us a great deal about the nature of sympathetic communication. Taken together, in fact, the studies on ambivalence and coolness and the abortion data provide a good insight into the nature of sympathetically communicated maternal emotions. A significant number of spontaneous abortions occur for no medical reason; the woman is fine physically and perfectly capable of bearing a child. Her problem is emotional, usually fear in one form or another. After studying more than four hundred spontaneous abortions, one investigator concluded that fear of responsibility and fear of bearing a defective child materially increased a woman's chances of abortions. In a second study, two other researchers arrived at the same conclusion. The only difference was that their subjects had other kinds of fears. They were afraid of being abandoned by their husbands, friends, family or physicians.

Fear, of course, has a biological basis, and it may well be that the neurohormones produced by maternal fear affect the intrauterine environment more powerfully than present research indicates. Even assuming that is true I doubt any new physiological findings can fully explain the cause of these abortions.

PHYSIOLOGICAL COMMUNICATION

Child

Until recently, it was assumed that the burden of physiologically sustaining pregnancy fell solely on the mother, but new evidence indicates that the child also plays an important role. According to Dr. Liley, for instance, it is the fetus who guarantees the endocrine success of the pregnancy and who triggers many of the physical changes his mother's body must undergo to sustain and nourish him prenatally.* So even at this stage the unborn child may have some control over his well-being, and this fact raises some interesting questions. Specifically, it raises the possibility that the unusually high rates of physical and emotional damage in the offspring of rejecting

---

* New studies show that the placenta, which is an organ of the unborn child, produces many hormones, such as estrogen, progesterone, chorionic gonadotropin, and others, which maintain the pregnancy. By producing these substances, the unborn baby actively participates in his own survival.

or unhappy mothers might not be due solely to harmful maternal hormones. It seems at least a possibility that if a fetus does have partial control over a pregnancy and senses himself in a hostile environment, in some instances he may withdraw his physiological support, thereby harming himself.

Mother

Anxiety- and stress-related hormones are the most obvious form of physiological communication from woman to child. Clearly, those anxieties that touch directly on the child, the pregnancy, the spouse or the woman's insecurities and inadequacies have the greatest impact on the fetus. *But only intense or continued maternal anxiety can be hazardous.* The woman who sometimes worries about bills or the weight she is gaining is certainly not putting her child at risk. The amount of hormones such minor concerns produce—if they produce any at all—are not going to affect an unborn child. What he cannot take is a continual assault of anxiety hormones. The danger here is not just to intrauterine bonding, either. As we saw in the last chapter, this kind of attack may also set the child's emotional thermostat at a precariously high level.

Smoking, excessive drinking, drug taking and overeating or eating improperly also qualify as forms of maternal physiological communication. (Psychologically, as I said before, they represent an indirect expression of anxiety.) The harmful changes these substances can produce in the unborn's environment may make him fearful, like smoking and, I suspect also, drinking—but then, he has every reason to be worried.

Alcohol is a case in point. It can maim, even kill the

child. Knowledge of its dangers in pregnancy goes back to the Greeks and Romans—who noticed that mothers who were heavy drinkers bore a much higher rate of deformed and sickly children. Only in the last decade or so have investigators found the scientific reason for this: Alcohol passes through the placenta as effortlessly as nearly everything else a mother eats or drinks. Exactly how it affects her child once it reaches him depends on the amount of alcohol he is exposed to and his stage of development.

I think the wisest policy is not to drink at all during pregnancy. If a woman does decide to, however, she should limit her daily consumption to, at the very most, two ounces of liquor or its equivalent. Anything above that puts her child in danger of falling victim to fetal alcohol syndrome (FAS). Investigators still do not understand all the mechanisms involved in this serious disorder, but they are quite sure of one thing: The more a woman drinks, the greater her child's chances of being born mentally retarded, hyperactive, with a heart murmur, or with a facial deformity such as a small head or low-set ears.

According to experts at the U. S. National Institute of Alcohol Abuse and Alcoholism, three or four beers or glasses of wine daily can cause one or more of these defects and six or more drinks a day can produce the whole horrendous gamut of deformities associated with FAS. A woman who drinks ten ounces of alcohol daily—or the equivalent of about six strong drinks—is playing Russian roulette with her child's life and health. At that level of consumption, his chances of being born seriously deformed are an even fifty-fifty.

Almost as critical as how much a woman drinks is

when. Those same experts warn that there are two periods of pregnancy when drinking is particularly perilous to the child. The first is from the twelfth to the eighteenth week, when his brain is in a critical stage of development; the second is from the twenty-fourth to the thirty-sixth week.

Cigarettes are another major hazard to the unborn. Smoking cuts the supply of oxygen available in the maternal blood and, without an adequate flow of oxygen, fetal tissue growth may slow. A woman who smokes one or two cigarettes a day is probably not seriously endangering her child (though, like alcohol, the best policy is abstinence), but the woman who smokes two packs a day probably is. According to recent studies, babies born to mothers who smoke forty or more cigarettes a day are smaller and in poorer physical condition than those of nonsmoking mothers. At age seven, children of smoking mothers tend to have more problems learning to read and a higher rate of psychological disorders than other youngsters. There is also growing evidence that a father's smoking may affect fetal development. West German investigators recently discovered that the unborn children of smoking men had a markedly higher rate of prenatal mortality than the babies of nonsmoking males. Why this is so is not quite clear. But toxicologist Helmut Griem believes smoking may produce subtle but potentially disastrous changes in male sperm.

Reports of the effects of caffeine on the fetus are less persuasive than those of alcohol or cigarettes. The handful of studies that have been done on caffeine in pregnancy have been inconclusive. The one partial exception is a recent report from the University of Washington, where investigators found a firm correlation between caffeine (whether in the form of coffee, cola, tea or cocoa) and certain birth disorders. The highest caffeine consumers in the study had the highest rate of babies with poor muscle tone and low activity levels. Are these effects short-term or are they harbingers of some serious and permanent health disorder? Dr. Ann Stressiguth, head of the team, says that vital question cannot be answered without further research.

Under the circumstances I think it would be wise for a pregnant woman to switch to a decaffeinated coffee and to cut down on cola or cocoa consumption. At the very least, the lack of caffeine will do her good (caffeine has already been implicated in high blood pressure, and recent evidence indicates it may also be a factor in breast cancer). But if a woman is so dependent on coffee or cigarettes that going without them would produce excessive tension, it is better to try to cut down rather than totally abstain from these substances.

The risks of drug taking in pregnancy have been so widely publicized that there is no need to dwell on them. Suffice it to say that the unborn is most vulnerable to their toxic effects early in pregnancy and that even small amounts of *any drug*, including common over-the-counter ones such as aspirin, can be harmful to him.

It may seem by now that everything a pregnant woman does, from taking a simple aspirin for a headache to having an occasional negative thought or tense moment, is going to affect her relationship with her child. This is not so. The material in this chapter has to be kept in perspective. *Occasional negative emotions or stressful events are not going to affect intrauterine bonding adversely.* The unborn child is far too resilient to be put off by a few setbacks.

The danger arises when he feels shut off from his mother or when his physical and psychological needs are consistently ignored. His demands are not unreasonable: All he wants is some love and attention and, when he gets them, everything else, including bonding, follows naturally.

Chapter Five

The Birth Experience

"Please, would someone shut off the lights," a gentle-looking woman asked in German. From the excited whispers and shuffling that followed, apparently everyone else in the Kantonspital in Basel was as anxious as I was for the film to begin.

Technically, what followed was something less than perfect. The images inexplicably went in and out of focus, and one had to strain to hear the voices clearly. Somehow, though, none of that mattered. Just by pointing the camera at new mothers and their children as they first set eyes on each other, the director had managed to create a genuinely moving film.

Thinking about this movie later, I realized it was not only a superb documentary on birth, but also an accurate depiction of our attitudes toward it. For most of its forty-five-minute running time, the film dealt with the mothers and their reactions. The camera lingered on their faces as they caressed, stroked and soothed their new children.

Since the subject of the film was childbirth, the babies
were bright-eyed and awake, but only brief shots of them
appeared. Clearly they were the supporting cast in this
particular drama; the real stars were their mothers.

This view is hardly unique to the film, of course. In
depicting birth largely from the mother's perspective, the
camera was simply reflecting what most of us think of
when we think of birth. It is the mother's eyes we see it
through; it is her joy that evokes our sympathies. We
assume her child feels nothing—that he is an innocent
bystander at the celebration. This is simply not true. For
his mother, for his father, his birth may represent an
unperishable memory, the fulfillment of a life-long
dream, but for the child himself, it is something much
more momentous—an event that imprints itself on his
personality. How he is born—whether it is painful or
easy, smooth or violent—largely determines who he becomes and how he will view the world around him.
Whether he is five, ten, forty or seventy, a part of him
always looks out at the world through the eyes of the
newly born child he once was. That is why Freud called
the pleasure and pain that accompany birth "primal emotions." None of us ever entirely escapes their pull.

To understand why, try looking at birth through the
child's eyes for a moment. By the end of his ninth month
in utero, he has become deeply aware of his universe; its
sensations, sounds, and sights are as much a part of him
now as his arms and legs. This is not meant mystically.
He is, in the most fundamental sense, at one with his
world and it with him. He has received messages from
his mother and through her from the world. They will
momentarily disrupt his tranquillity and begin laying the
foundations of his emotional life. As I said before, mini-

mal anxiety messages will help the unborn develop his sense of self. Except in rare cases, though, brief disquieting messages of "ambivalence" or "anxiety" from an otherwise caring mother will not affect him.

Birth, on the other hand, is the first prolonged emotional and physical shock the child undergoes, and he never quite forgets it. He experiences moments of incredible sensual pleasure—moments when every inch of his body is washed by warm maternal fluids and massaged by maternal muscles. These moments, however, alternate with others of great pain and fear. Even in the best of circumstances, birth reverberates through the child's body like a seismic shock of earthquake proportions.

One moment he is floating blissfully in a pool of warm amniotic fluid, the next he is suddenly thrust into the birth canal and the beginning of a trying experience that may last many hours. For most of that time, maternal contractions will push and pinch at him. What the full force of a contraction feels like can only be guessed at, though some recent radiological studies show that as each contraction closes in on the child his arms and legs flail wildly in what looks very much like a painful reaction.

Almost as unnerving is the end point of his birth. When the child finally nears the vaginal opening his still fragile skull may suddenly be seized by two steel forcep tongs and his six-, seven- or eight-pound body pulled forward at a force equal to forty pounds of tension on his neck. Or he may find inserted in his scalp a tiny metal electrode lead from a fetal cardiac monitor. Even if he manages to avoid both these hazards, he will likely soon find himself in a cold, noisy, harshly lit room, surrounded by a group of strangers who clutch, probe and pull at him.

Meanwhile his mind is recording every feeling, gesture and movement. Nothing escapes his attention now. Even the most minute details leave indelible memory tracks, though the child will rarely be able to recall these memories spontaneously later. Almost none of us can. Birth produces a kind of amnesic effect; there is good reason to believe that it does so because of the oxytocin (the female body's principal hormone for inducing uterine contractions and lactation) secreted by the mother during labor and birth. Recent studies (which will be examined more closely in Chapter 10) show that oxytocin induces amnesia in laboratory animals, so it may be that the presence of this hormone accounts for the fact that so many birth memories slip from our conscious recall.

Certainly we know birth memories exist, and we also know they can be retrieved, if properly prodded. Dr. Penfield's studies demonstrated that, but his work dealt with early memories. Dr. David B. Cheek, in contrast, has focused his attention specifically on birth memories. In a remarkable clinical experiment done several years ago, he took four young men and women he had delivered during his years as an obstetrician in Chico, California, put them under hypnosis, and asked each to describe how his or her head and shoulders were positioned at birth. Positioning was selected as a measure of the reliability of birth memory because Dr. Cheek knew there was no way his subjects could know the answers beforehand. Information like this rarely finds its way beyond the obstetrician's delivery notes, and the delivery notes of these young men and women had been under lock and key in Dr. Cheek's files for more than two decades.

They were the test's corroborating proof. In every case what the hypnotized patient told Dr. Cheek was confirmed by what he found in his files later (he was careful not to consult them beforehand for fear of leading the subjects on). Each man and woman accurately described how his or her head had been turned and shoulders angled at birth, and also the way he or she was delivered.

What makes Dr. Cheek's work so significant is its larger implications. If a child can remember something as minuscule as how his head was turned at birth, what about more traumatic events? Specifically, what about the memory of being trapped in the birth canal, or being unable to breathe for several seconds, or of being thrust out into the world weeks, even months before term? What happens when these physical hazards are compounded by maternal anxiety, fear or hostility?

The work of Dr. Cheek and other investigators now makes it possible to answer these questions with some precision. It is even possible to plot the various "birth-risks" and their psychological effects on the child in chart form, complete with graphs and bars. From animal studies and clinical investigations I have formulated five major categories of birth-related psychological hazards, which, though still tentative, incorporate the best and most recent available data.

At bottom, in the chart's lowest psychological risk category, would be simple, uncomplicated vaginal births. While my own empirical evidence shows that a large majority of people born vaginally are outward-going, optimistic and trusting, I cannot point to any one study and say, "There, that proves what I've said." But the reports that have been done—and they are largely on animals—indicate that an uncomplicated vaginal birth does confer important emotional advantages.

In a study done at the National Institute of Neurological Disease and Blindness in the early 1970s, investigators found that vaginally born monkeys (the monkey's reaction to birth is closest to man's) were much more active, responsive to others and quicker to learn in the five days after birth than Caesarean-delivered monkeys (whose mothers had been given a local anesthetic to rule out the dazing effect of heavier drugs). How the Caesareans would compare with the vaginal group two, three or five years later is another matter. Many minor birth-related disabilities disappear with time. However, among my own patients, I have noticed what may be one long-term effect of a Caesarean birth: an intense craving for all kinds of physical contact. This is probably because the Caesarean's delivery deprives him of the sensual moments a vaginally delivered baby has during birth—both the excruciating pain and the extreme pleasure. These sensual feelings are the forerunners of adult sexuality, and the surgically delivered person may never quite overcome their loss. For these reasons, Caesarean deliveries would place slightly higher than vaginal births on the risk chart.

On top of them, or about a third to a half of the way up the chart, I would place breech births, which occur in about one out of every thirty-five deliveries. While most breech babies go on to lead perfectly normal lives, studies indicate they run a slightly higher risk of developing learning problems later in childhood. Matching the academic progress of 1,698 Indianapolis youngsters, investigators found that the children who failed at least one grade and required academic remedial help were much more likely to have had a breech birth.

At about the same level of risk as breech births I would place minor, momentary umbilical cord difficulties, such as a cord pinch or a cord loop that quickly corrects itself.

Neither is life-threatening, but each can disturb the child's breathing for a few terrifying seconds. For that reason, I suspect they leave long-term psychological marks that tend to be quite specific; each disability, in fact, has its own internal logic. For example, babies who have had cords accidentally caught around their necks at birth tend, as children and adults, to suffer from a higher rate of throat-related problems, such as swallowing difficulties or speech impediments.

This was true of a man I treated who had been a severe stutterer since the age of six. Very early in his therapy it became clear that his father was a key piece in the puzzle. As a boy the patient had been criticized about his speech unmercifully by his father, which, of course, only made it worse. As therapy progressed, however, it gradually emerged that this criticism was only one of several important contributing factors; the man also had a history of throat-related problems. In one session he remembered having a painful series of tonsil infections between the ages of three and five; in another, he recalled being born with an umbilical cord looped around his neck.

Because his birth records were not available, I was not able to verify this recollection. But in the weeks following the emergence of his birth memory another, more meaningful form of corroboration presented itself: The man's stutter gradually began to disappear.

On top of cord difficulties or about half to three quarters of the way up the chart in the direction of critical problems would go premature births. These can vary in degree of severity. A few days' prematurity will be of little consequence; a few weeks will matter more, and a few months can be both physically and emotionally devastating to the child.

On the most minor level, I have noticed that many of my prematurely born patients tend to feel rushed and harried all the time. I suspect the feeling that they will never, ever catch up is a direct result of their prematurity. They began life rushed and now, many years later, they still feel that way.

There are others like a youngster I'll call Ricky Burke, whose prematurity leaves deeper psychological scars. Ricky's case came to my attention in a roundabout way. One of the local Toronto radio stations asked a therapist at my center, Sandra Collier, to do a special two-part broadcast on dreams, nightmares and their significance. Sandra had done quite a bit of work in this area—particularly on the connection between dreams and forgotten birth memories—and she mentioned this toward the end of the first program. It was one of those odd coincidences; a listener hears a strange voice on the radio and suddenly her life and her family's lives are changed.

In this case, the listener was Kathleen Burke, and hearing Sandra discuss how dreams can express unconscious birth memories made her think about her son, Ricky, and his birth. For the past several years, Ricky had been tormented by horrible, frightening nightmares. Night after night, just after falling asleep, he would thrash about cursing, but cursing in a vocabulary far beyond the powers of any six-year-old. Stranger still was the yelling and screaming that followed. Sometimes he would also talk of an odd light and speak in what to his mother sounded like a foreign language. None of the doctors to whom the Burkes had taken Ricky could help; they would either pronounce his condition undiagnosable or prescribe a medication that turned out to be useless.

After listening to Sandra's broadcast, however, Mrs. Burke found herself thinking again about the circumstances of her son's birth. She had had a very difficult labor; Ricky was born prematurely, nearly dead. Gradually, as her mind began focusing on that night, other details emerged—her overtired doctors had cursed. A priest was called in to administer last rites to Ricky. As his mother was remembering all this, suddenly, everything fell into place. Ricky's nightmare grew out of his birth memory; his swear words were those he had heard the doctors using; his language, the priest's Latin. It all made perfect sense, Mrs. Burke said, when she called during Sandra's second broadcast to tell her about Ricky.

"Lucky" may seem an odd word to apply to Ricky Burke, but considering the difficulty of his birth, he *was* lucky to escape so lightly. A delivery complication like Ricky's belongs in the last quarter of the chart. Problems in this category include life-threatening instances of prematurity (births that were at least two months early, for example); cord difficulties that bring the child within an inch of death; placenta previa, which can block his exit from the uterus at birth; and eclampsia, a potentially menacing form of maternal hypertension.

The psychological problems often associated with these disorders are equally severe—schizophrenia, psychosis and violent antisocial and criminal behavior. As a matter of fact, evidence in the scientific literature overwhelmingly favors the view that physiological complications at birth predispose the individual to a wide range of injuries; from psychological damage to organic brain damage. For example, in a study of 33 schizophrenic youngsters, investigators found a 40 percent rate of birth complications of all types. The rate for their mentally healthy brothers and sisters was, in contrast, only 10 percent.

More dramatic still are the results of an especially good study by Dr. Sarnoff A. Mednick, director of the Psykologisk Institute in Copenhagen. In the early 1960s, Dr. Mednick began following a group of more than 170 youngsters who had been marked as possible candidates for schizophrenia because their mothers had the disease. Dr. Mednick wanted to know how many of the children would ultimately develop it and, more importantly, why.

Within a few years, he had an answer to the first part of his question. Twenty of the young men and women had, by then, become schizophrenic. Looking for clues as to why they, and not the others, had succumbed, Dr. Mednick found what he thought were some significant similarities in their backgrounds. He noticed that many of the schizophrenics' mothers had been institutionalized earlier for their disease. He also found that early in their school years, many of the 20 had been branded as troublemakers by their teachers. But the one fact that leaped out at him was the similarity in the 20 victims' birth histories. Seventy percent had suffered one or more complications at birth or during their mothers' pregnancies. Turning to the records of the children who evidenced no schizophrenia, Dr. Mednick found a different but, in its own way, just as telling a figure. Only 15 percent had had any kind of complications during pregnancy or birth.

Equally dramatic are the results of a second study by Dr. Mednick. His subjects this time were men who had committed violent crimes. Again he found the one common denominator to be birth history—15 of the 16 most violent criminals had had extraordinarily difficult births. (The 16th had an epileptic mother.)

Many—perhaps even the majority—of these violent and painful births are either entirely preventable or, in cases where they aren't, their effects can be materially reduced. Sometimes this can be accomplished by providing more of the sophisticated technological medical care that modern obstetrics has come to specialize in, sometimes by providing less of it. And at all times, by paying very close attention to the emotional state of the woman about to be wheeled into the delivery room.

How she feels at that moment has an enormous influence on how she delivers. If she is relaxed, confident, and looking forward to the birth of her child, chances are very good her delivery will be simple and trouble-free. If she is racked with doubts and worries and is in conflict about the prospect of becoming a mother, the risk of complications rises accordingly.

We know that not just from the delivery records, but from what are, in a sense, the eyewitness accounts of the soon-to-be delivered infant. During these hours the child is, among other things, acutely aware of his mother's feelings, and often his or her memory of those maternal emotions may surface decades later, spontaneously or in therapy.

One of the most arresting accounts of this nature came to me from a middle-aged woman I had been seeing for about a year. It surfaced one afternoon toward the end of what had been an emotionally exhausting session for both of us. The woman was talking about something unrelated when suddenly she stopped in mid-sentence and her facial expression changed. Before I had a chance to ask her what was wrong, she began describing how frightened her mother had been during her birth, how she felt that fear had made her mother withdraw into a protective ball. "I knew she wasn't going to help me be born," the woman said, "and I was scared because I'd have to do it all by myself." Another patient, a slightly younger woman, delivered by Caesarean, had an equally dramatic birth memory. She recalled her mother's dread as the surgeon prepared the incision: "I could feel her terror as the knife began cutting across her stomach."

One of the problems with these accounts—from a strictly scientific standpoint—is that they are very often difficult to corroborate. Either the patient's mother is unavailable or, for one reason or another, cannot or will not recall the particulars of the birth. However, there is a great deal of hard research to support the notion that such positive emotions as confidence and anticipation and such negative ones as deep-seated anxiety can affect the delivery process.

A University of Michigan study found that anxious women labored much longer than calm women. More definitive still is another report from the University of Cincinnati. In this one, the researchers did not simply look at anxiety per se, but at different kinds of anxieties and stresses and the effect each had on labor time and uterine contractions. Overall, ten psychological factors were tested; the three that prolonged labor most and produced the most inefficient contractions were, respectively, "Attitude toward Motherhood," "Relationship to Mother" and "Habitual Anxieties, Worries and Fears." In other words, the women who had the easiest deliveries also had the fewest ambivalences about motherhood, the fewest conflicts with their own mothers and were the least anxious generally. One other reassuring finding from this study is how little effect normal apprehension has on laboring time or uterine contractions.

Many studies show that birth complications also occur more frequently in seriously troubled women. In one conducted several years ago at Brown University, the subjects were fifty women, half of whom were rated as troubled before birth by investigators, and half as normal (that is, looking forward to birth). After their deliveries, a group of obstetricians unconnected with the study reviewed each woman's delivery record, and what they reported back to the investigators was staggering.

All the troubled women had had at least one complication during delivery, from relatively minor ones—bearing a child with a bruised nose—to major ones—in several cases, prematurity, and, in two others, stillbirths. The data on the women rated "normal" was in its own way just as spectacular. Not one had had any complications or problems delivering.

Of course, this does not mean that every severe maternal stress will necessarily harm a child. Still, who knows how much physical and emotional pain we—and by we I mean such health professionals as obstetricians, psychiatrists, midwives and nurses—could prevent simply by starting to pay as much attention to the pregnant woman's emotional health as we do to her physical health?

One other measure that could probably decrease the physical dangers of birth and certainly reduce its psychological hazards is equally simple. All it involves is using drugs, forceps, fetal monitors, Caesarean sections and the other elaborate technology that has gradually come to dominate birth with more restraint and wisdom.

In cases where mother or child is in danger, this technology can literally mean the difference between life and death. That is what it was designed for—emergencies. Unfortunately, most obstetricians use the technology at their disposal routinely on women who don't need it. Eighty percent of American women receive at least one drug during delivery, 30 percent of the infants born vaginally are dragged into the world with forceps, and 15 percent of all deliveries are done by Caesarean section.

How much direct physical harm these and modern obstetrics' other high-powered paraphernalia do to mother and child is hard to say. Virtually every authority agrees birth is better and safer without drugs. Do they actually harm the child? Most studies indicate that, yes, in the short run, they do. Infants whose mothers have had general anesthesia during delivery tend initially to be more sluggish and have less motor coordination. These manifestations may persist many years after birth.

Caesarean sections pose the same kind of problem. Virtually every authority, again, agrees that birth is better, and safer, without surgery. Yet that has not stopped the rate of Caesareans in the United States from climbing 200 percent in the last two decades. An important impetus for this alarming increase has been the introduction of the fetal cardiac monitor, which provides an ongoing reading of the child's heart rate and breathing during birth. That, say obstetricians, has helped them spot the baby in trouble sooner and do something more quickly to assist him—usually, performing a Caesarean section. They *claim* that with that and the fetal monitor they can save children who a few years ago would have died during birth—but they cannot really prove it with figures. I agree with those who think that the rise in Caesareans is needlessly exposing increasingly large numbers of women and their children to the hazards of surgery.

Forceps are another dangerously double-edged obstetrical tool. Given the fact that even the slightest slip of the metal tong or a bit too much pressure can leave the baby's brain permanently damaged, is it wise to use them in nearly a third of all births? A growing number of experts think not, among them Dr. Cheek, who believes it is the laboring woman's anxiety that causes her to tighten her pelvic muscles, which, in turn, leads to the excessive use of forceps. If mothers were better prepared for childbirth the number of forceps injuries could be drastically reduced. He cites tension and migraine headaches as problems that are often traceable back to forceps deliveries.

That these conditions might be related to forceps occurred to Dr. Cheek under unlikely circumstances. He was taking a cruise when one of his fellow passengers was struck by a severe headache. The man had a history of headaches that always hit in the same place—the forehead just above his right eye. The passenger was sure they had been triggered by a bad eye infection he had suffered as a boy.

Yet he was proved wrong. Under hypnosis, he briefly described how the eye infection occurred, but then quickly drifted back in time to his birth, which from his account had evidently been a harrowing one. He remembered his mother's cries and then felt his head explode with terrible pain.

In response to a question, he said his forehead just above the right eye hurt most, but he could also feel something sharp at the back of his neck toward the base of his skull. To Dr. Cheek, this sounded very much like a high-forceps delivery or, rather, an attempt at one that had misfired. The forceps—and hence, the pain—should have been located at the sides of the infant's head, behind the ears. That they were not, and that the forceps tong causing the most pain was pressing against his forehead, seemed to explain the original sources of his headaches.

Dr. Cheek might have left that ship with nothing more than a hunch and an interesting story but for a chance encounter on the dock with his new acquaintance's mother. No doubt the last thing she expected when she arrived to meet her son's ship was to find herself being questioned about his birth, but when Dr. Cheek explained why he wanted to know, she said that his birth had, indeed, been very difficult. She was in great pain throughout it. For a few moments, he had been dangerously close to death. What saved him—and just barely, she said—was the high-forceps delivery her obstetrician had executed in desperation at the last moment.

Of course one story, even one where every small detail has been independently confirmed, does not make a case. Dozens of things from simple tension to brain tumors cause recurring headaches. We do not know how prevalent forceps injuries are because we have done very little research on the long-term consequences—not just of forceps but of all the other routinely used obstetrical practices and procedures from ultrasound to episiotomies.

Obviously, there will be times when these procedures are absolutely essential. But they are used routinely now, and that is clearly uncalled for. As Dr. Leboyer has noted, it would be hard to think of a more frightening introduction to the world than the one obstetrics has, however unwittingly, devised for this generation of children.

More often than not, babies are delivered under harsh lights in a cold stainless steel room, filled with gloved and masked strangers. Once born, they are usually snatched from their frequently dazed and drugged mothers and deposited unceremoniously in a nursery filled with other screaming, frightened children.

The amazing thing is not that this system is now being attacked, but that it took so long for parents and doctors to realize how detrimental it was for the newborn and his parents.

Everything we have learned in the past decade tells us we could not have devised a worse way of birth if we tried. Yet many children in the western world continue to be born in a setting that might be appropriate for a computer, but that is wildly inappropriate for the birth of a human being.

One small but relevant example of a practice that continues despite all we have learned is the separation of mother and child immediately after birth. Many obstetricians argue fervently that it is necessary because what mother and child need most after the exhausting ordeal of birth is rest and plenty of it. But all the recent work on parent-infant bonding shows that this is untrue—that what mother and infant require and want most in these minutes and hours is not sleep or food, but to stroke and snuggle and to look at and listen to each other. Hundreds of studies have demonstrated this over the past several years.

Let me return for a moment to that movie I mentioned earlier. What I and the rest of the audience at the Kantonspital found so fascinating was how the director had managed to capture this bonding on film. The mothers and children in it were not drugged or dazed or exhausted. They were old and loving acquaintances who could not wait to set eyes on each other.

Bright-eyed and alert, the babies began searching for their mothers immediately after birth. None of them could see further than a foot or so, thus anything as remote as a mother's face was far beyond their range. But each time a mother spoke, her child turned or tried to turn his head in the direction of her voice. As soon as each baby was laid on its mother's stomach, he would eagerly begin inching his way up—in a kind of swimming motion—toward her breast. Perhaps the most startling thing, though, was how little these children cried. Until the nurse arrived to take them away, they were perfectly quiet and content.

I think the audience was even more struck by the mothers' behavior. All of us were health professionals— doctors, nurses, psychologists, psychoanalysts—familiar with birth: many of us had performed deliveries. But I do not think any of us had ever seen women slip as effortlessly into the role of motherhood as these women were doing on the screen. You could see it in their actions and gestures. Just the way they hugged and cuddled their babies spoke volumes about motherly love. The director of the movie, a young German woman named Sigrid Enausten, said later that one of the things that impressed her most during the filming was the way the women talked to their babies. Their voices grew softer, their words simpler; even the verbs they used changed. It was all clearly instinctual, because the moment a doctor or nurse addressed a mother, the adult tone automatically returned to her voice, and her language became more complex.

Ms. Enausten also said she was surprised at how unconcerned these women were about their child's sex. That is usually the first question a new mother asks, but these new mothers were so thrilled just looking at their babies and touching them that they did not notice or think to ask whether they had had a boy or girl until half an hour, sometimes an hour after birth. It was enough simply that the child was there, safe and well. Another thing that Ms. Enausten noticed was how confidently the children were handled. Many of the women were first-time mothers, but none was nervous or reticent about holding her child. Each woman held her child the first time like it was the thousandth.

We do not know how much the children gained from this gentle birthing experience because they were part of a film and not a clinical study. But the results of several recent studies suggest that it is likely these babies did benefit immensely. These reports examined several different kinds of birth experiences and their influence on a child's subsequent intellectual and emotional growth. What they found is that the children who learn the most quickly and seem happiest had bonded with their mothers after birth. In other words, pretty much the same kind of birth the infants in the film enjoyed.

Furthermore, we know from clinical studies that the infant's memories of his first primal attachment with his mother continue to affect his sense of emotional security years later. That has been demonstrated in the pioneering bonding work of Drs. Marshall Klaus and John Kennell. Those whom the team refers to as "bonding infants" grew into much more self-sufficient, outgoing youngsters than children who were taken from their mothers immediately after birth.

There is another classic series of studies that are

among the most original and insightful ever done on mother-infant attachment. The investigators, a husband-and-wife team from the University of Wisconsin named Harry and Margaret Harlow, wanted to determine what would happen if you took a group of monkeys right after birth and put them in a cage with artificial surrogate mothers. To find out, the Harlows designed two types of what were, in essence, monkey versions of a scarecrow. One had a wire-framed body, a wooden head, and a nipple protruding from one of its wire breasts, which supplied milk. The second mock mother was identical except that the Harlows draped a terrycloth towel over her body (the nipple protruded through a hole in the towel). That simple addition, it turned out, made all the difference in the world to the monkeys.

The infants caged with the wire mother drank as much milk and gained as much weight as those who had a terrycloth mother. But whenever the monkeys were given free and equal access to a wire and a terrycloth mother, all of them spent their time with the terrycloth version. They clung to her and hugged her as if she were a real mother—something that never happened with the wire mothers. One day, when the Harlows sent a tiny wind-up mechanical toy marching noisily through their common play area, all the frightened little monkeys immediately ran to the terrycloth mother. She had earned all this trust and affection simply because she had been draped with terrycloth.

If even baby monkeys have this kind of extraordinary sensitivity to touch and feel, what about the three-day-old human child? What goes on in his head as he lies in an impersonal, noisy nursery surrounded by strangers? How will absence of all meaningful human contact during these critical hours affect him later, affect his feelings toward his mother, his father and, one day, toward his own·wife and children? Can there be any doubt that he would feel better if he stayed with his mother more and by himself less?

Chapter Six

The Shaping of Character

It should be clear by now that birth is one of the most profound experiences we undergo. The games we play as children, the entertainment we enjoy as adults, even our sexual interests are, in one way or another, birth-related. To take one small but very common example: Why does a child spend hours rocking gently back and forth on a playground swing? Swinging is not a game or a skill he is taught by parents or teachers. Children are drawn to swings instinctively because swinging reproduces the gentle swaying motion of the womb. The adult who thrills at the magician's ability to pull a rabbit from a hat is responding to the same impulse. The rabbit's mysterious appearance from nowhere reminds him unconsciously of his own birth. This symbolic re-creation of man's magical emergence from the womb is why magic has always had such a powerful tug on the human imagination.

Many of our little idiosyncrasies can also be explained

in terms of birth. We all know people who, no matter how nasty the weather, won't wear hats, turtleneck sweaters, scarves or other restricting clothing around their necks. While this behavior is usually shrugged off as quirky by their friends, I think its origins lie in a tumultuous birth experience. Most infants present frontally, which means the head and neck are the two body areas that receive the greatest battering during birth. It is not hard to understand how someone who has had a particularly painful delivery might develop an aversion to head and neck wear later.

These kinds of long-term influences are what I had in mind earlier when I said that part of us always looks out at the world through the eyes of the newborn we once were. Birth and prenatal experiences form the foundations of human personality. Everything we become or hope to become, our relationships with ourselves, our parents, our friends—all are influenced by what happens to us in these two critical periods. Having examined how uterine experiences shape us, now I'd like to explore how birth does.

The long-term influence of early birth memories emerges very clearly in the second part of the study I conducted among my patients. It shows indirectly that if we are happier or sadder, angrier or more depressed than other people, it is, at least in part, a result of the way we were born, although very few specific correlations between birth itself and such feelings as anger and depression emerged; most of the links were with sexual attitudes.

Our sexual tastes say a great deal about us generally. A strong ego and high self-esteem, for instance, are almost invariably associated with healthy sexual preferences, while a battered or fragile ego and self-loathing are equally likely to produce strong, sometimes dangerous sexual predilections. A good example of this is the link the study found between induced labor and sexual perversion. A person who gets sexual delight out of tormenting his partner is unbalanced generally; this was confirmed by the fact that induced labor not only correlated with sexual sadism but also with a masochistic personality.

In this kind of birth labor is brought on by a chemical derivative of oxytocin which is fed intravenously into the mother. This causes her uterus to contract and eventually push the baby out. However, if the synthetic oxytocin is stopped, the contractions often stop as well, and the labor can be a very long and frustrating ordeal.

Many women who have experienced an induced birth (and it is important to point out that most induced labor is performed at the obstetrician's suggestion or insistence) describe the experience as something that is "done" to them. They feel that the contractions do not originate inside themselves, but that they are imposed on them from the outside. As a result, they lose control of their bodies and it is much more difficult for them to push in rhythm with their contractions. The mother is not in harmony with her body, and she is not in harmony with the baby at all.

The baby, who is not ready to be born, is thrust out of the uterus by its contractions, but gets very little help from the mother if she cannot push during her contractions or if she is pushing between contractions. Also, because the mother cannot push as effectively, and because induced labors tend to be longer than spontaneous labors, the baby is often eventually pulled out by forceps.

This type of birth is most unsatisfying for both mother and child. Labor has been imposed upon both of them; neither was physiologically ready. They were not able to work together in the birth process, and my findings seem to support the view that this lack of harmony during birth can delay or impede later mother–child bonding and affect the baby's personality development.

Induced labor is also a bad idea because it is physically dangerous. "Every fetus reacts differently to it," says Dr. Edward Bowe, director of Clinical Obstetrics at Columbia Presbyterian Medical Center in New York and a leading expert on synthetic forms of oxytocin commonly used to induce labor. "You can't predict who's going to take off and do well and who is going to have tetanic [prolonged] contractions, during which time the fetus may suffer brain damage or possibly even die from a lack of oxygen."

The dangers Dr. Bowe describes may explain why the people in the study whose births had been induced also had a higher rate of delivery problems. And that put them at double jeopardy, since measured independently, a difficult delivery—for whatever reason—carries its own particular emotional, physical and sexual risks.

Many mothers experience strong sexual feelings during birth; and many of their children also have moments of intense pleasure as they pass down the birth canal. This is the child's first physical contact (remember, he has been submerged in a protective pool of amniotic fluid for the past nine months), and it leaves an indelible impression on him.

Now, suddenly, his entire body is being squeezed and rubbed. His skin is being directly stimulated for the very first time. Together with this stimulation, he is also experiencing pain. The uterine contractions exert a great deal of pressure on his body, especially on his head, neck and shoulders.

This combination of pain and pleasure leaves a lasting mark on his sexual inclinations. Generally speaking, the more pleasure the baby experiences during birth, the more likely he is to develop normal sexual attitudes later.

If the data from my study are a reliable guide—and I believe they are—birth experiences play a vital role in shaping sexual inclinations. The mutual stroking, hugging, kissing, whispers and murmurs common to adult sex have many parallels in birth and subsequent bonding behavior.

Caesareans are a case in point. The caressing and massaging the baby receives as it passes down the birth canal represent a first encounter with sensuality and, however diffuse or unfocused, the quality of that feeling leaves a permanent mark. It is, in a very real sense, a forerunner of adult sexuality; so, in a different way, is the total absence of it. That is why Caesareans often have sharply different sexual (and even physical) attitudes.

Surgical delivery deprives a child of the physical and psychological pleasures a vaginally born infant experiences. Removed from his mother's uterus in an operating room, he gets no massaging or caressing. The feelings birth stirs in him often sound a discordant note. Physically, the Caesarean has trouble with the concept of space. Knowledge of his body proportions does not come naturally to him. He does not seem to know where he begins or ends physically, so he is prone to be clumsy. Sexually, the effects are manifested in a hunger for body contact. The Caesarean demands, indeed requires continual stroking and hugging. Given the way he was born, it is not hard to see where his cuddle-hunger comes from.

Pain is the second vital element in all births. Intermingled with pleasure, it creates a sharp contrast for the infant. Nothing in his experience has prepared him for the pain and anxiety he endures as he is shoved down the birth canal. Despite the magical interludes of pleasure, he feels under active assault. The legacy of this journey—with its bewildering and harrowing contrasts —leaves a profound mark on all of us. Our most enduring cultural and religious symbols reflect that influence: Both the distinctions between Heaven and Hell and the expulsion of Adam and Eve from the Garden can be read as birth parables, and so can many of our most powerful myths. How we are born may even influence how we die. There is a remarkable similarity in the accounts of people who have been clinically dead for a brief period. Scientist-author Carl Sagan thinks this resemblance may actually be a reflection of the commonality of the birth experience.

Sexually, these contrasts leave a mark in the form of ambivalence. Men express this ambivalence differently than women, and some of us feel the ambivalence more acutely than others, since the ratio of pain to pleasure in the birth balance varies from one person to the next. At its root lies a subconscious desire to re-experience the joy and tranquility, the safe place we once possessed in the womb. In men this longing often expresses itself in mindless promiscuity. Endless sexual conquests are really veiled attempts to re-enter and recapture the serenity of the womb. But since by its nature this is an unrealizable goal, inevitably each compulsively repeated sexual encounter ends in disappointment.

Though superficially similar to promiscuity, in women the desire to enter the womb takes the quite different form of hugging and cuddling. Since both are usually available only as part of sex, many women—especially single ones—become promiscuous to get the holding they want. The intensity of this desire varies greatly, as the birth balance does. Some women do not feel it in any direct way; in others the yearning to be held and gently rocked back and forth is almost palpable. Several years ago, one young woman described the desire to psychiatrist Marc Hollander as a "kind of ache. . . . It's not like an emotional longing for some person who isn't there," she said; "it's a physical feeling." Dr. Hollander was interviewing her as part of a study on women and holding, and his results illustrate how deeply this need—and, hence, the influence of birth—runs. Of his thirty-nine subjects, slightly more than half (twenty-one) told him they had used sex to entice a man to hold them. Most of the women asked to be hugged first; the men, however, wanted sex, so to get one the women had to agree to the other.

A second, quite different study shows the lengths to which some women will go to satisfy their longing for holding. The subject of this report was illegitimate pregnancy. The question under study: Why do certain women repeatedly become pregnant out of wedlock? The investigators expected to hear a lot of complex emotional reasons, but the one that kept turning up was the desire to be held. Of the twenty women interviewed—all of whom had three or more illegitimate pregnancies— eight said sex was the price they willingly paid for being held. Most described intercourse itself as something "merely to be tolerated."

Anger is another birth legacy we all share. It is a widely accepted psychological principle that pain produces anger and, since even the best births involve pain, it is inevitable that all of us are left with a subconscious residue of primal anger. That is perfectly normal. A danger arises only when that residue is large and unexpressed. This may occur because of an unusually painful birth— but even a relatively normal delivery can produce fury in an infant if the pain confirms what he has already begun sensing in utero—that his mother is rejecting or ambivalent. That is what happened to Kristina, who spurned her mother's breast. For her and infants like her, the profound experiences of delivery tip the birth balance toward pain. They often remain irreducibly furious and, lacking an acceptable outlet, very frequently turn the anger inward against themselves. A common psychological phenomenon, unexpressed anger accounts for a number of emotional problems, among them psychosomatic diseases such as ulcers and, even more commonly, depression.

Though a host of factors, including physiological ones, may lie behind depression, primal anger often plays a central role. An example is a man I'll call Ian, whose case was reported at a recent American Psychiatric Association meeting. Ian was a severe chronic depressive. Under hypnosis, his doctor explained during a panel discussion, Ian said he felt as if he were being pushed up and down in an elevator, and that made him feel alternately angry and depressed. Analyzing the image later, both Ian and the doctor concluded that the rhythmic, pulsating movement of the elevator symbolized sexual intercourse. But Ian could take this no further. Nor could he explain the alternating anger and depression he felt at the very thought of the hypnotic experience.

At their next session, Ian came up with the answers. He was not sure why, he explained, but something in the elevator image—maybe the anger—connected with his mother. He had never gotten along with her and, thinking about the image and the emotions it produced, he began to suspect it was related to his feelings toward her. So he called and asked her on the spur of the moment if she had had sex with his father while she was carrying him. "Yes," she replied after a brief hesitation. "Right before you were born." She insisted that it hadn't been her fault; his father had come home drunk one night and had forced himself sexually on her. Three hours later, she told Ian, she went into labor. "Listening to this story," Ian's psychiatrist said, "I felt a little like Newton watching the apple drop. Everything suddenly fell into place." I think it would for even the most skeptical psychiatrist. Until the day he unraveled its origin, Ian had internalized his anger at his mother for her "betrayal," which accounted for his deep and prolonged depression.

We may still not understand all the ways such primal emotions as anger and ambivalence work themselves into childhood and adult psychiatric disorders, but once we open up the interconnections between birth-related primal feelings and later adult personality characteristics, more and more connections between them become apparent. I have noticed a correlation among my own patients, for instance, between eating disorders (including obesity) and birth and the events immediately following it.

From the beginning, food acquires important psychological meanings for us. Some of us use it as a substitute for sex, some for love, and others to help keep frustrations in check. This process starts with the newborn. How often he is fed, the quality of his food, and the care with which he is fed, all take on meanings that influence his attitude toward food later. For example, if a mother feels good about herself and her baby, and if she has joyful memories (conscious and unconscious) about her own early relationship with her mother, she will probably feel good about breastfeeding. As a result, her child is likely to develop a healthy, well-balanced attitude toward food. Breastfeeding itself does not miraculously produce this attitude. If it makes a woman feel uncomfortable or if alcohol or cigarettes are contaminating her milk, the child is likely to form an altogether different impression. Learning he can trust neither the provider of his food nor its quality, he may come unconsciously to associate food with negative feelings, which as an adult may lead him to suffer from any of a variety of eating disturbances.

An unnaturally abrupt severance of the food-mother bond may also cause problems later. Since food, in the mind of the child, has come to be associated with love, security and tranquility, it represents to him a source of special emotional magic full of rich and nurturing connotations. When it abruptly vanishes because the mother is too ill or busy to continue feeding him, he is going to be visibly and profoundly distressed. He may spend the rest of his life trying to recapture that lost love with a knife and fork.

This is not inevitable, of course, because no one incident, however important, shapes us irrevocably. As we move through life we continue to change and grow. But events such as birth and weaning, which until now have been viewed as "objective," physiological phenomena, produce definite and long-lasting effects on the personality of a child. We must learn how to make the most of these opportunities.

Chapter Seven

Celebrating Motherhood

A great many damning things have been written lately about the mechanization of birth, and with good reason. The transformation of what should be a supremely human moment into a celebration of medical technology is demeaning and, in many cases, self-defeating. Recent studies and statistical analyses leave no doubt about that. But to my mind, one of the most devastating criticisms of the way we deliver children now is Dr. Michelle Harrison's stark account of a birth she witnessed one night as a house physician in a small, suburban New Jersey hospital. That the delivery room happened to be in New Jersey is incidental. It could just as easily have been in any other American hospital—or a French, German, English, Canadian or Italian one—and that's what makes Dr. Harrison's account so compelling.

"In the delivery room," she wrote, "the patient . . . was doing well when I arrived, mildly pushing, groaning, but not screaming. . . . She had already successfully labored

127

many hours alone and I thought she would enjoy the rest. . . . I gowned, gloved, [then] checked her. She was fully dilated and would deliver quickly. I draped her. . . . Then, the anesthetist arrived—a young man, arrogant—and seated himself at her head. He placed a mask over her face and told her to breathe deeply. He reassured her it was almost over. She had only two or three contractions to go. I asked him what he was giving her. He ignored my question. . . . Minutes later he decided to answer, but I couldn't hear what he mumbled. It didn't matter, though, because at that moment the obstetrician arrived. The anesthetist deepened her sleep to await the scrubbing and gowning of the OB. . . . The OB stepped in, ignoring my presence. He and the anesthetist began speaking to one another. The patient was now choking on the tubes in her throat. Her labor had stopped; the table had been tilted forward so the OB could look down at the spreading lips. Then, they spoke with contempt. The anesthetist was saying angrily that the woman was gagging. The OB that she had stopped being of any help to them—she wasn't pushing, her uterus wasn't contracting. Forceps were unwrapped, applied, and with deepened anesthesia the infant was lifted up and out of his mother's womb by the iron clamps about his head. He was blue and listless, but soon recovered with oxygen and some slapping.

"The obstetrician and the anesthetist went on talking while the patient was sewn up. They spoke of partners, of Puerto Rico, of vacations, weather, etc. The event of birth was lost to . . . standard male locker room talk."

Obviously this is not a desirable way to bring a child into the world or to treat an adult woman. Modern obstetrics can and must do better. The revolution in prenatal psychology has put us within grasp of a new birthright for our children—one that can make an immense difference to them, to us their parents, and, ultimately, to society. We have the knowledge, we have the understanding. We only need to apply them.

Since everything a woman thinks, feels, says and hopes influences her unborn child, the kind of prenatal care she receives and the delivery alternatives she is offered should begin reflecting that fact. I am not suggesting that there is one best kind of birth; what works wonderfully for one woman may not work at all for another. But the various alternatives offered to an expectant mother should, without exception, be humane, effective, safe, meaningful and appropriate. Birth is a celebration of life and hope, not a pathological disease state. Therefore, modern obstetrics must return to basics—to "baby catching," not surgery; to treating pregnant mothers as persons and not "patients." It should allow a woman and her family a voice in all decisions concerning labor and delivery. To ignore an expectant mother's wishes and desires, as so often happens, is unconscionable. She has earned the emotional triumphs of pregnancy and she has every right to enjoy that vital, integral part of her womanhood. An obstetrician has no business denying it to her by playing God.

As Dr. Harrison's story makes disturbingly clear, however, many obstetricians are unwilling to share the responsibility of childbirth with the mother. They were taught in medical school that birth is largely an engineering problem, and they seem determined—no matter what their patients' wishes or what new research shows —to continue treating it that way. Fortunately, there are some exceptions, and while still not large, their numbers are growing. So too are the number of new family-centered approaches and programs, which can help deepen and enrich the meaning of pregnancy and birth. However, no one technique—no matter what its adherents may say—is suitable for everyone. An obstetrician, friends and family can provide advice and guidance in choosing, but in the final analysis the decisions are the parents' alone to make. Selecting among the various alternatives not only brings them peace of mind, but it can provide the kind of reassurance that benefits both them and their child.

This is not to say that there still won't be the occasional twinges of anxiety. Even the best prenatal program available will not silence all doubts; these are a normal part of every pregnancy and a woman would not be human if she did not have a few. But fears about stretch marks, her figure or how she will stand up to the pain of labor can be allayed through discussion with an obstetrician, midwife, friends or a prenatal counselor. Knowing that a concern is universally shared brings a measure of relief in itself. So does familiarity: A labor room will not look nearly as intimidating or frightening if it has been visited beforehand, and neither will the doctors and nurses on the obstetrical floor if one has had the opportunity to meet them before the big day.

A sense of perspective also helps—particularly when it comes to pregnancy's effect on the body. As a mother of four, English prenatal counselor and anthropologist Sheila Kitzinger knows something about this subject firsthand. Even so, she is continually amazed by the results each time she asks her prenatal pupils to draw pictures of themselves pregnant. Even the happiest, most exuberant expectant mothers see and draw themselves as dumpy, unattractive creatures. (The fact that most pregnant women realize their situation is temporary distinguishes them from the high-risk mother, who believes she is going to be rendered permanently unattractive. I will expand on this subject below.) As Dr. Kitzinger rightly points out, this is a view few males share. The allure of the pregnant woman's body, with its full, flowing lines, gives many men a sense of real sexual pleasure, and women should be aware of that.

Sometimes things you normally wouldn't think of—such as living space—can also create anxiety. One study showed that cramped quarters significantly soured feelings toward pregnancy; the more room a husband and wife had, the happier they felt about the pregnancy. Couples in homes felt better than couples in apartments and so on. Obviously one way of dealing with this is by making present living quarters more spacious. Another is by moving. The best time to make a move is before becoming pregnant, but if that is not possible, trying to find a home or larger apartment in the same general area is a wise course. As we have seen, moving in pregnancy poses some peril, but there is evidence that what upsets women is not the move itself, but the move to an entirely new locality.

Work also affects a woman's perception of pregnancy. I have found that women who are their family's sole means of financial support often make the poorest adjustment to pregnancy. In a study conducted by Dr. Helmut Lukesch, these women were frequently the most angry and resentful, which is understandable. In general, though, working at home, working in an office, or not working is, in a sense, beside the point. What matters is the sense of accomplishment and worth a woman gains from her work, because the way she feels about herself is going to affect the way she feels about her unborn child.

In the final analysis, the normal, well-adjusted woman who *feels* good about her pregnancy will make the transition to motherhood smoothly as she makes every other critical transition in her life. The women (and children) in danger are those who enter pregnancy already in emotional turmoil, and unfortunately many of them go unnoticed and unaided. Psychological screening is still not a routine part of prenatal care in most places. Nor are many obstetricians, midwives or prenatal counselors sensitive to the psychosomatic aspects of pregnancy. An expectant mother's nutrition, weight, heartbeat and blood pressure are minutely monitored, but almost never her psyche. Unless a woman's distress is so obvious that those around her cannot ignore it, she is unlikely to be referred for psychological help.

Inevitably, that means a large number of women who could benefit significantly from counseling never get it. The effects of this shortcoming are there to see—in the studies on stress, and in the studies on pregnancy and birth complications. To be fair, though, many mothers who are emotionally at high risk do seem perfectly normal; and in fact many of them were normal until pregnancy ignited some dormant psychic conflict that had been established long before. A woman comes to pregnancy with a given history, a formed ego and a practiced coping style. If and when her ego becomes threatened in some unforeseen way or her coping style collapses under the emotional pressures of pregnancy, then danger arises —and then, for her sake and, even more, for her child's, she should seek help.

The emotionally high-risk woman tends to fall into one

of three categories. The first, and probably most common, is the woman caught in an unsatisfying relationship. Pregnancy has a way of delineating the parameters of a marriage with intimidating clarity. All the little cracks and fissures that could safely be ignored before suddenly begin looking imposing. Doubts, long buried, spring up: What kind of mother will she make? Is he reliable? Do I want to be a father? Couples find themselves asking new questions of themselves and of each other and, if the answers they get are not satisfying, their relationship can deteriorate precipitously—with enormous consequences for their unborn child. The best time to ask such questions is *before* pregnancy, but if they arise during it, a couple should immediately seek some form of marriage counseling.

One other significant relationship in a woman's life that may also affect her pregnancy and delivery is the one she had with her mother. A child learns her first lesson about mothering from her own mother. She is her daughter's initial and most influential role model. If she is a strong, supportive mother, it is likely her daughter will become one as well. If she is not, if she is uncomfortable or anxious in the role, or feels inadequate, her child runs a greater risk of feeling the same way when she becomes pregnant, and that can lead to serious physical as well as emotional problems. One recent Swedish study found that what I will call "unhappy daughters" had a noticeably higher rate of birth and pregnancy complications than happy daughters.

Of course many women who related poorly to their mothers have normal pregnancies and grow into happy, confident mothers themselves. What such a history does do, however, is raise the risk of incurring obstetrical complications; for that reason, such women should try to work out their conflicts before becoming pregnant.

Finally, there is the woman beset by fears and anxieties that are unusually intense and morbidly specific. Her concerns are not random and they are not easily laid to rest. In study after study, she is the one who exhibits the deepest degree of fear and dependence. She is at the mercy of her husband, her obstetrician, her mother, her friends. There seems to be no decision, however small, she can make alone. Her fears are often wildly irrational. First and foremost, she is concerned about what pregnancy is doing to her looks. This is not a casual or passing concern, but a near obsession: Each stretch mark becomes the harbinger of doom; she will never be slim or attractive again; pregnancy has maimed her beauty forever. Her other obsession is the health of her child: Without any medical evidence, she is somehow sure he will be born deformed or irretrievably injured.

These feelings can produce a wide range of potentially dangerous problems. One researcher, for instance, found that such women often have difficulty bonding with their infants after birth. A recent report from the University of North Carolina shows they also run a materially higher risk of incurring birth complications. Women in this study who had the longest labors, the most forceps-attended deliveries, and bore babies with the lowest Apgar scores* also scored highest in testing on dependency, fears for self and fears for baby.

As I mentioned earlier, the key word with regard to

---

* The Apgar score is based on five tests performed one to five minutes after birth. It measures the newborn's pulse, breathing, muscle tone, reflex irritability and color (blue to pink). A score of seven or above is considered good, four to six only fair, and below three so poor that resuscitation is necessary.

these anxieties is *intensity*. It is one thing to be consumed by such fears—and a therapist can help deal with that—and another to be legitimately concerned about one's self and one's child. A sensitive, understanding physician can help a woman deal with these worries. Next to your husband, he is the most critical figure in your pregnancy. Remember that delivery room scene Dr. Harrison described at the beginning of this chapter? It was not chance that brought the young mother's labor to a screeching halt. Strapped to the delivery table, in the middle of a painful labor, she was at her most vulnerable when her obstetrician walked in. Had his attitude been more humane, the rest of the birth would have proceeded as smoothly as Dr. Harrison had expected earlier in the evening.

Who delivers and how the woman feels about him or her makes that much difference. It is a difference that should be explored carefully beforehand. The first step in making a choice is deciding who is most suitable, a family physician, an obstetrician or a midwife. For the physically high-risk mother, that decision has already been made. Her illness or her child's will dictate the use of an obstetrician. A woman who feels uncomfortable without a physician or equates a delivery without one with second-rate care is also better off with a doctor. The peace of mind his or her presence will provide could be important to her later during pregnancy and delivery.

The best way to find a compatible doctor is through friends who have recently given birth. They will be able to provide the small but important details about personality and philosophy that are not included in the recommendations hospitals and county medical societies make. The next step is a personal interview, and it is best to interview several doctors before settling on a final choice. Be direct, and don't let yourself be intimidated by the white-coated figure on the other side of the desk. Remember, you are—or should be—the one who makes the final decisions.

Ask about treatment philosophy. Is the physician going to be delivering the baby or are you? Also find out what kinds of deliveries he or she is most comfortable doing—will the doctor assist at a natural birth or only at a medicated one? And what about his or her (and the hospital's) rules on fetal monitoring, ultrasound, anesthetics, episiotomies, shaving and the use of enemas? Will your husband be permitted in the delivery room; will your baby be allowed to remain with you after birth? And if your child is born premature or ill, will you be able to visit him in the hospital's pediatric intensive care unit? The way these questions are answered is just as important as the answers themselves. You should be comfortable with your doctor's style; and, more important, you should trust him or her. No matter how appealing, or how great his or her reputation, if your doctor doesn't elicit a sense of trust in you, don't use him as your birth assistant.

This also applies to midwives. Although they have a long and venerable history, only since the late 1960s have they re-entered the medical mainstream in significant numbers. That very newness may make some women uneasy. But I think a midwife offers some important advantages. For one thing, her viewpoint toward birth is likely to be more sympathetic and humanistic. Unlike a physician, whose disease orientation trains him or her to see birth as a potentially pathological state, the midwife's training teaches her to view it as a normal biological event.

She is a specialist, too, but in natural births, and the methods she employs reflect that fact. Episiotomies, fetal monitoring, prepping, all the normal paraphernalia of a medical birth are usually absent at midwife-assisted deliveries. Her orientation makes her more receptive to innovations. Usually, she is just as comfortable with, say, the Bradley method as she is with Lamaze, and as comfortable assisting in a birthing room or maternity center as in a hospital delivery room. Another of her advantages is accessibility. She has more time to answer questions and is usually really interested in supporting her patient emotionally. A young woman I will call Marsha can attest to that. Her first child was delivered by an obstetrician, her second by a midwife. The midwife, said Marsha, made a difference. "Toward the end of my labor, while I was pushing, she leaned over and said, 'Help push your baby out.' She used the word 'baby' and she kept using it. The doctor had just said, 'Push, keep pushing.' He made it sound so mechanical. The word 'baby' made it real. It reminded me that I wasn't there pushing as an abstract exercise. There was a real baby trying to come out."

A midwife brings more than sensitivity to her task, and that is particularly true of a nurse-midwife. Just to qualify for nurse-midwife training, a woman first must be a registered nurse and have at least one year's experience in public health as well as one year of in-patient hospital service. Usually the training itself takes anywhere from eighteen months to two years; during that time the midwife will normally participate in over one hundred births. Added to the deliveries she attends once she has graduated, that often gives her as much or more experience in managing a normal pregnancy than even a busy obstetrician.

One of the other important choices a woman faces early in pregnancy is how she will deliver her child. When I was a resident at Harvard in the early 1960s, there were essentially only two delivery options available, medical vaginal or Caesarean. All births took place in a hospital. Fortunately that is no longer true. The women who came of age in the late sixties and early seventies entered their childbearing years with very definite ideas about the meaning of birth and who its chief beneficiaries should be. For the most part, they have been able to impose those ideas on obstetrics. Today, several types of natural childbirth preparation, as well as a wide range of delivery options, are readily available.

As I have said before, I have no quarrel with the use of medical or Caesarean deliveries for the physically high risk mother or child. For normal deliveries, however, I strongly favor some form of natural childbirth. It puts control where it belongs—with the woman and her husband. The scale is human; there is none of the technical overkill that so often accompanies a medical birth. Most important, the child is allowed a gentle, graceful entrance into the world. And given everything we have learned recently about the psychological importance of birth, that fact alone makes a natural childbirth worthwhile.

Just as important as the kind of delivery a woman chooses is the way she prepares herself for it mentally and physically, and the best place to get the right kind of preparation is a prenatal class. These not only provide instruction in pregnancy, labor, birth and infant care; they also serve as a kind of extended family where new parents can meet and share their hopes, fears and expectations. Choose your classes carefully. The various prenatal programs that offer them all have their own distinct philosophies of childbearing.

A woman who wants a structured delivery, for instance, would probably be very comfortable with the Lamaze method. Its emphasis on discipline and mastery are well suited for someone who likes to be in control. The ideal Lamaze woman is, in fact, like a superbly trained athlete who has disciplined herself to perform under intense pressure. The analogy is not an idle one. She trains with the rigor and dedication of an athlete and she approaches birth as if it were an Olympic event she is intent on winning—winning, in her case, being defined as remaining drug-free, awake and playing an active role in the delivery. Classes stress the control of such feelings as fear or pain, which might get in the way of that goal. The Lamaze woman is schooled to handle these feelings in an orderly, disciplined way. She learns how to ease contraction pain by relaxing her muscles at will, how to distract her attention through breathing exercises and how to pace the delivery by braking herself psychologically and physically.

To help her achieve her goal, she must enlist the aid of another person, preferably her husband, who attends classes with her and acts as her emotional coach during the delivery. In the late stages of labor, for instance, he assumes command of the baby's passage down the birth canal, instructing his wife when to push and when to relax.

Another popular form of birth preparation is the Bradley method. The emphasis is on everyone—mother, father, baby and doctor—doing his or her part. One of the Bradley instructional films, *Happy Birth-Day*, catches this spirit nicely. It features a boisterous soundtrack, a beaming mother as star and a supporting cast of T-shirt wearers—the doctor's identifies him as "Baby Catcher," the father's as "Coach." Bradley preparatory classes stress the importance of feeling rather than physicality. Husbands and wives are encouraged to discuss their marital and sexual problems openly in class as well as their expectations about parenting and how they see themselves fitting into their new roles. Nutrition is heavily emphasized. Some pelvic and abdominal exercises are taught, too, but, unlike Lamaze, Bradley does not stress rigorous mental or physical conditioning. The technique is best described as "relaxed." Women are urged to leave themselves open emotionally during childbirth, to express and embrace what they feel, rather than try to intellectualize and master it.

All this makes Bradley a unique and, in many ways, ideal way to have a child. Like Lamaze, however, it is not suited for everyone, including some first-time mothers. Bradley leaves a woman pretty much on her own during birth. Without knowing how she will react when she is actually in labor, a first-time mother may find that lack of structure a bit scary. A more logical candidate is a woman who wants to be able to set her own delivery goals, but who, having already had one child, is also confident enough of her reactions in delivery to turn the freedom Bradley offers to her own advantage.

The last of the big three forms of natural childbirth, the Dick-Read technique, is also the oldest. Modified considerably since it was introduced in the late 1940s, it still remains the least ideological and most straightforward. Thoroughly down-to-earth, it has none of the élan of Lamaze or the open, laid-back quality of Bradley. Adherents of the Dick-Read technique like to think of themselves as practical, placing a great deal of emphasis on the value of education and its ability to banish the fears and tensions that produce many of the pains of childbirth.

Dick-Read courses do teach coping skills, such as breathing exercises, but education is their first priority. Women learn what to expect during delivery, how to help themselves and how to accept support from others. Dick-Read also stresses what happens after birth; couples often learn as much about the problems and challenges of parenting as they do about childbirth. It offers, in short, a pragmatic, sensible and nonjudgmental approach to birth. The Dick-Read technique does not require the degree of personal commitment other types of training do. I think a woman who would like to explore the idea of natural childbirth in a nondogmatic environment will find its classes a good place to start.

For all their differences, the one thing Lamaze and Bradley do have in common with Dick-Read is an open-ended approach to delivery. A woman is free to choose the Leboyer method or what has come to be called a "Gentle Conventional Birth," a kind of hybrid that combines aspects of a natural and a medical birth. Either one works with all three types of preparation; of the two, however, Leboyer is probably the more popular— though not among obstetricians—and is certainly the better known. For the past few years, it seems every magazine I have picked up has had a story on the way it has changed birth.

Briefly, a Leboyer delivery is characterized by dim lighting, immediate skin-to-skin contact between mother and newborn, delayed cutting of the umbilical cord, and massage and bathing of the infant by his father. Leboyer enthusiasts claim that this kind of "gentling" makes the child's passage into the world as positive and enriching as possible. While I agree that it does, I think the benefit comes not so much from Leboyer's "special effects" as from the facts that the delivery is natural and compassionate, the mother is enthusiastic about it, and it allows the parents to begin bonding immediately with the newborn.

Other forms of natural childbirth can also supply those three factors, as the results of a recent Canadian study show. After the publication of Dr. Leboyer's book *Birth Without Violence*, obstetrician Murray Enkin suddenly found himself swamped with requests from patients for Leboyer-type deliveries. However, at that point the method had not yet been tested in a scientific manner. So, with the help of several colleagues and his patients (who were chosen because they were expected to have uncomplicated deliveries), he decided to do his own study.

He randomly selected one group of patients to deliver according to Leboyer. Another group delivered by a gentle conventional method, which might best be described as Leboyer without the trappings—the baby is born naturally and drug-free, but the lights are not dimmed, his umbilical cord is clamped a bit earlier and he is not bathed or massaged; he also does not have immediate skin contact with his mother. Reviewing the results, Dr. Enkin found that, with one notable exception, there were no significant differences in outcome between the two groups. Women in both groups had about the same rate of complications, which, incidentally, were low, and were nearly as likely to ask for an anesthetic to ease their labor pain. The one exception was the much shorter first-stage laboring times of the Leboyer mothers—a fact Dr. Enkin thinks was due not to the method of delivery, but to the women's enthusiasm about it.

No important differences emerged among their children, either. Initially, the Leboyer babies were slightly more active and energetic, but by the third day the other group caught up. More significant was Dr. Enkin's failure to find any evidence to support claims that the Leboyer method of delivery is more soothing for an infant. Despite the bathing and massaging, the Leboyer babies cried as readily as the other infants. His conclusion that both delivery methods were equally safe and effective seems to me thoroughly justified, as does his assertion that what really matters is that the birth be tailored to each couple's and each baby's individual needs.

That involves more than just selecting an appropriate form of delivery. *Where* a woman decides to bear her child can be just as important as the method of delivery she chooses. The setting should make her feel comfortable and relaxed, be appropriate to the act of birth, and also be safe. More and more mothers believe that while a hospital delivery room meets the last of these requirements, it does not meet the first two. These women have been turning to alternative birthing places. One of the most popular *and* controversial of these is the home.

To home-birth advocates, that is where birth rightly belongs. And I agree with them that a home birth has real advantages. Living with birth—and death—on a daily basis gave our ancestors a much surer and saner grasp of life's rhythms and revelations than we have. The problem is, are home births safe? In a few years, as more data begin to accumulate, we should have a much clearer idea, but at the moment there are so few hard statistics on its safety that as much as I would like to, I hesitate to recommend it. Those studies we do have on it are unsatisfactory. A recent one conducted in Oregon illustrates why. On the face of it, the report seems to be a clearcut condemnation of home births. The investigators found babies born at home had nearly double the death rate of hospital-delivered infants. On closer inspection, though, the study turns out to be full of flaws. For one thing, a large number of the home births were apparently unattended, and even the home-birth movement's most fervent advocates oppose unattended deliveries. For another, the study only looked at *reported* home births, and all indications are that a significant number of such births go unreported. Still, the very one-sidedness of the figures should not be ignored.

Two alternatives that attempt to combine the medical protection of a hospital with the relaxed atmosphere of a home are in-hospital birthing rooms and maternity or birthing centers. The in-hospital birthing rooms are usually private or semi-private rooms that have been curtained and painted to add a touch of warmth. Inevitably, they never look as warm as the hospital brochures make them sound, but for all that, they have some distinct advantages as a birth setting. One is that the couple, not the hospital, gets to set the rules. Within reason they can have whom they want in the room during the delivery, and there is almost no limit on how long the baby can stay after birth. Many women find that fact alone makes an enormous difference.

"What bothered me most about my first baby's birth," one woman told me, "was having him whisked away immediately. I was still wide awake and I wanted to hold him for a while. But they wheeled me right back to my room, which was unlit (my roommate was trying to sleep and didn't want the light on), and after my husband went out to make some phone calls, there was no one to talk to. So there I was, thirty minutes after having a baby, sitting in a dark room alone, with nothing to console me but a bag of lollipops I had brought along. I felt terrible."

At her midwife's recommendation, that woman elected to have her next child in a birthing room. "Everything was so much more peaceful and joyful the second time," she recalled. "There were no machines around, my husband was able to stay with me, and I kept the baby for several hours after delivery." She even found her labor was different. "It went much easier; afterward I couldn't believe how great I felt. After the first delivery I was a physical and emotional wreck for a month."

Independent maternity centers are not yet as widely available as birthing rooms, but their numbers have grown rapidly over the past few years and I think they will continue to do so. Of all the alternatives, to me these centers seem to come closest to providing an ideal birth setting—a warm, home-like atmosphere, combined with good medical backup. For example, at one of the best-known birthing centers, the Childbearing Center in New York City, a woman gets a living room, a kitchen, an outside garden and two bedrooms—one for herself and one for her support person.

At maternity centers rules and interferences tend to be minimal. Immediate family members are permitted to attend the birth and the infant is normally allowed to remain with his mother for an hour or so after birth. Medically, the centers are not designed to be a match for a big hospital. They only admit low-risk mothers (to minimize the chance of emergencies) and are staffed largely by nurse-midwives who supply most of the care, including doing the deliveries. Centers usually have an obstetrician on call who handles emergencies, and a pediatrician, who examines the baby after birth.

Their aim, like that of the other settings and techniques discussed in this chapter, is to rescue birth from technology and restore it to its rightful place in the family. I believe that this will benefit the mother and her child and, in the long run, all of us.

Chapter Eight

The Vital Bond

Her contractions started one April evening while she was setting the table for dinner. At first the pain was so slight —really more a vague gnawing than a pain—that she thought it might be her imagination. Her delivery date was still a month away; it could easily have been a false alarm. By the time she was being wheeled into the delivery room three hours later she knew it wasn't. The bursts of pain were coming in five-second intervals now. She was ready to deliver, so ready there would not even be time for an anesthetic to ease her pain. The birth would have to be drug-free.

That was not the way she had planned it, and for a woman normally upset by the unexpected that might have been deeply distressing. But watching her child being born had a deep effect on her. In the hours and days afterward, she found herself elated. She felt better about herself than she could ever remember feeling and much closer to Ann—as the baby was named—than she had been to her first child. Somehow, being able to hold and cuddle her child—which she had been too drugged to do with her first-born—had dissolved her anxiety.

"Mrs. B.," as Dr. Lewis Mehl called this woman in one of his papers, is real; so is her story and so, too, were her feelings and thoughts after the delivery. Stroking, hugging, bonding with a child does make a critical difference. As little as an hour spent together after birth can have a lasting effect on both mother and child. Study after study has shown that women who bond become better mothers and their babies almost always are physically healthier, emotionally more stable and intellectually more acute than infants taken from their mothers right after birth.

Bonding is that central. Everything a woman does and says to her infant after birth—all the seemingly purposeless cooing, hugging, stroking and even looking—have one specific purpose: to protect and nurture her child. In exactly what ways this system works we do not know, though new evidence indicates that, in this period at least, much of what is called motherly behavior is biologically regulated.

This possibility was raised by an intriguing study done at Rutgers University. Experimenting with the body chemistry of female rats, an investigator there noticed something strange. The animals' maternal instincts were dependent on the flow of a certain specific hormone. It appeared in their bodies toward the end of pregnancy, and as long as it was present the rats made ideal mothers. That, in itself, was an important finding.

What the researcher wanted to find out, though, was how the flow of this hormone was controlled. He discovered that the regulatory mechanism was the presence of the rat pups. If they were taken away immediately after birth, the hormone vanished from the mother's body and along with it, her maternal instinct. Once gone, nothing could restore that instinct, including the return of her offspring.

Animal studies are, in themselves, rarely definitive, but there is excellent reason to believe this one may be. We already know a newborn's presence is biologically critical to his mother in at least two important respects. His cries stimulate her production of breast milk, and the touch of his skin against her breast releases a hormone that reduces post-delivery bleeding. Is it too farfetched to suggest that his presence may also release her maternal instincts? Most of the biological and behavioral evidence suggests not.

Child abuse, which occurs far more frequently among youngsters who were born prematurely, is a case in point. Many authorities believe that the isolation of premature babies in special pediatric units for weeks, sometimes months after birth has a devastating psychological effect on their mothers, making them more likely to physically abuse their children later.

Furthermore, the available evidence indicates there is a specific period immediately after birth when bonding or the lack of it has a maximum effect on both mothers and children. Studies disagree somewhat on its length— some limit it to the first hour or less, others to the first four or five hours. A study done by bonding pioneer Dr. John Kennell and his team indicates that its uppermost limit is well under twelve hours. He and his colleagues found bonding immediately after birth drew a mother closer to her child than bonding that began twelve hours after delivery. The differences appeared almost immediately. Within a day or so, what I will call the early-contact mothers were already holding, fondling and kissing their babies noticeably more than the late-contact group.

This does not mean late-contact women will make bad mothers. A woman's maternal feelings are too complex and personal to be entirely reducible to biological reactions. The thousands of intimate moments that fuse mother and child together throughout life are also important. My point is simply that bonding gives a woman an important edge. And as I have said before, any edge is vital because of the total pattern or attitude it helps form. Dr. Kennell's team, for instance, noticed that even elementary tasks such as diapering and feeding give non-bonding women more difficulty. A case in point is one young woman I know whose child was whisked away immediately after birth; it was nearly twenty-four hours before she saw him again. At first, that had not bothered her terribly, she said, because in the hospital she felt close to him. A month later, her attitude had changed. She felt uncertain that the baby belonged to her; the baby seemed like a stranger. This woman was sure that eventually a bond would grow between her and her child, and I reassured her that one would. However, it would have grown sooner if she had been able to spend some time with her baby after birth.

Almost invariably, women who bond early behave differently. The same differences turn up in study after study whether the subjects are white, black or Oriental, rich, poor or middle-class, American, Canadian, Swedish, Brazilian or Japanese. Up to three years later bonding mothers still are acting more attentive, enthusiastic and supportive. Looking at one group of women a year after their deliveries, Drs. Kennell and Klaus found they still were touching, holding and stroking their children more. When the researchers visited them again a year later, the women were now *talking* differently to their children. Very few of them yelled or shouted. A mother might gently suggest to her child that it was nap time or that he ought to pick up his toys, but it was always done with implicit respect; rarely was an order issued. The investigators were also struck by the way the women's talk seemed to envelop the children in a rich, nurturing swirl of soothing, ego-building words. Simply by the way they were addressed, these toddlers knew they were loved and wanted.

Speech like this is not taught in a prenatal class and it cannot be learned from Dr. Spock. It comes naturally to happy mothers. Like the new mothers in the movie I mentioned earlier, these women were acting entirely unconsciously. Their choice of words, their speech patterns and their tone of voice were completely spontaneous.

Nature has gone to great lengths to design a bonding system that fits the newborn's needs in very precise ways. She not only dramatically alters the behavior of an adult woman who has already lived twenty to twenty-five years or more (an alteration, by the way, Freud insisted was impossible), she alters it in exactly the ways and for the length of time that suits the baby best. To thrive emotionally, intellectually and physically an infant needs the special kind of loving contact and care that only bonding fully develops in his mother.

The baby also is prepared to play his part in bonding. Unable to feed, clothe or shelter himself, the sounds he makes and, I think, even his looks are specially designed to elicit a loving, protective response from those who can feed and clothe him. Not long ago, scientist Carl Sagan remarked on the special tug large-headed, small-figured creatures seem to exert on us. Dr. Sagan thought it might be because an outsized head subconsciously reminded us of the brain's predominance over the body. I suspect it is more likely that we are programmed to respond lovingly to all such babylike figures. We may think what is endearing about cartoon characters like those in "Peanuts"— Charlie Brown and Linus for example—is their stoic humor, but I wonder if we are not really responding to the vulnerability of these figures with their outsized heads and small bodies?

Certainly, on seeing her newborn for the first time a mother will instinctively reach out to hold him. The most natural reaction in the world, like every other aspect of bonding it also fulfills a specific and essential need of the child. At birth, love is not only an emotional requirement but a biological necessity for a baby. Without it, and the cuddling and hugging that go with it, an infant will literally wilt and die. The name for this condition is *marasmus*, from the Greek word for "wasting away," and during the nineteenth century it killed more than half the infants born; until the early years of the twentieth century it was responsible for nearly 100 percent of the deaths in foundling homes. Quite simply and brutally, these children died for lack of a hug. Today there are fewer cases of marasmus. Unfortunately, though, there are still too many neglected babies among us. Doctors call them failure-to-thrive infants.

Even a little caring produces small miracles in a love-starved child, as one investigator demonstrated in a study on low-birth-weight infants. Their slower-than-normal growth rates are usually blamed on organic problems, slight brain damage being the most frequently named culprit. This researcher thought there might be another explanation. He noted that in the first weeks of life, these babies are often isolated in pediatric intensive care units. With their high-powered technology, these units can do everything for a child except hold or love him.

And that is what the researcher thought was wrong. So he selected a particular group of infants in his unit and asked the staff to stroke them for five minutes every hour around-the-clock for ten days. Five minutes is not much time and a nurse is not a mother, but for all that, the stroking produced dramatic results. These babies gained weight faster, grew more quickly and were physically more robust than the infants who had not been touched.

A few years after this study, another team ran a somewhat similar test, making what proved to be one critical change. Instead of pediatric nurses, they used real mothers. Initially, that did not produce any major surprises. Like most other bonding babies, the infants thrived. But when the investigators examined these children four years later, another major difference had emerged. On the average, the stroked youngsters scored 15 points higher in IQ tests than the children who had not been touched.

Of course what happened to these youngsters at one, two and three was also critical. Intelligence is not set in granite at birth and it does not develop in a vacuum. It requires continual stimulation by the child's family, friends and teachers. By joining mother and child, bonding supplies not only someone who understands and loves the baby but also an ally who can provide the infant with the stimulation he needs to expand emotionally and intellectually. This is a lot harder than it sounds.

Only a very narrow spectrum of stimulation registers on newborns. A woman who wants to amuse, entertain or interest her child must choose her forms of play very carefully. And without ever quite knowing how or why, that is what she does; for just as bonding increases her feeding and diapering skills, it also seems to increase her emotional sensitivity. A bonding mother often knows intuitively what will hold her child's attention.

Much of what a newborn learns in the first days of life, he learns through his eyes. Lying in his cradle, he is forever turning his head this way and that, searching his horizon for someone or something to spark his interest. He wants to be entertained, excited, possibly even to learn, but because his range is so severely circumscribed, the visual stimulation must be of a very special order. If it is too intense, he will feel overwhelmed and withdraw; if it is not intense enough, he will not notice it. A face at rest, for instance, will not arouse him; it is too low-key and, at this stage, its features have not acquired the emotional resonance they will later—even if they belong to his mother. But flaring eyebrows, rolling eyes, a head thrown back in mock surprise—in other words, all the somewhat exaggerated, slightly silly expressions bonding mothers make instinctively—turn out to fit his stimulation spectrum perfectly.

Japanese, American, Swedish, Samoan and nearly all other mothers play with their babies in exactly the same way. They choose forms of play that fit a newborn's intellectual spectrum precisely. Moreover, evidence indicates that all the seemingly random, silly behaviors mothers use in play are not random or foolish at all, but a number of quite distinct games, each with its own set of rules, regulations and time frame; each is designed to broaden the child's intellectual abilities.

"Mugging" is one example of an early and fairly simple game. But within a month or two an infant will already be demanding something more challenging and exciting. Even at seven or eight weeks of age he has distinct ideas about what makes a good game, how it should be played, and for how long. One of his favorites is what bonding expert Dr. Daniel Stern calls "punch line behavior." It is so named because watching women and their babies at play reminded Dr. Stern of a comedian telling a long, elaborate, funny joke to a receptive audience. It begins with mother and child revving each other up. The comedian's part is played by the mother; she does something silly—maybe crosses her eyes. The baby smiles or moves his arms and legs excitedly—a signal he wants more. That encourages the mother to do something sillier still. Gradually each of them grows more and more excited until, finally, the game reaches a climax similar to the punch line of a joke. Both "break up" in laughter—the mother often literally, the child figuratively—his excitement threshold peaks and he kicks and waves his arms and legs wildly. Then after a pause, much like the breather a professional comedian gives an audience between jokes, the game begins again.

That is, if the child wants it to. If he is bored, and he gets bored quickly at this age, he may signal that it is time for a new game by turning his head away, lessening the intensity of his gaze, or by refusing to smile, which are the ways he expresses his wishes and feelings at this point.

He is also equally adept at sensing other peoples' feelings toward him. Eyes tell him a lot, but touch tells him even more. Stroking, petting and holding are an infant's information source—a way of making some important judgments about the other person, and more importantly, about that person's feelings toward him. If an infant is approached in a cool, disinterested, suffocating or angry manner it tells him he is unloved and, perhaps, even in some danger. Alternately, if the holding is warm and supportive, he picks up the feelings of this person and reacts accordingly.

Bonding mothers somehow seem to know this, too. Watching new mothers pick up and cuddle their babies, I have been struck time and again by the effect bonding has on a woman's grasp. Whether they are more confident or more comfortable, bonding mothers almost invariably embrace their children differently. The women in the movie I mentioned earlier are an excellent example. Though most of them were first-time mothers, they held their children with assurance and authority. None were nervous or fidgety.

I was reminded of them again recently, while watching a young woman who had not had a chance to bond trying to feed her baby for the first time. As the nurse handed her the child she smiled, trying to hide her nervousness. For a few moments, she shifted the child uneasily from arm to arm looking for a comfortable position. Then finally, finding one, she picked the bottle up and clumsily thrust it into the baby's mouth. What struck me most was the expression on her face at that moment: Watching the infant gulp greedily from the bottle, her eyes began narrowing, her jaw tightened, and she looked grim and determined. To be fair, her reaction was entirely unconscious and I am sure if anyone had put a mirror up to her she would have been as surprised by her expression as I was. She could not help herself, though. The sight of milk dribbling down her child's chin upset her.

In contrast, feeding, particularly breastfeeding, comes

as naturally to bonding mothers as every other aspect of infant care. Matching the breastfeeding experience of bonding women and non-bonding women, a Seattle investigator found some striking differences. By the eighth week after delivery all but one of the non-bonding women had given up breastfeeding as simply too much bother. The bonding women, on the contrary, found the experience so exhilarating they all breastfed their babies until they were at least eight weeks old.

Much the same thing happened among a group of Brazilian women. Two months after their babies' births, three quarters of the bonding women were still breastfeeding. Among the non-bonding women, only one quarter had continued breastfeeding beyond the second month.

Keep in mind that what these studies were measuring was the effect of bonding on the length of time a woman breastfed, not the psychological benefits of breastfeeding itself. Scientifically, that has yet to be established in a conclusive way, though I strongly believe that one day soon it will be. Nature is very economical. Each of her systems is designed to fulfill many different needs; there is no reason to think breastfeeding is any exception to this rule. If it confers very real physiological benefits— and breast milk's effects on a child's health and immunity are considerable—it is also likely that it confers psychological ones. This, however, is no reason for a woman who doesn't breastfeed—because she can't or doesn't want to—to feel guilty. What really counts psychologically is what emotions are communicated to the infant during feeding. A child can feel loved whether he is breast- or bottle-fed.

A father's love is every bit as complex and important

as a mother's. Given a chance, a man can be just as "motherly" as a woman: protective, giving, stimulating, responsive to his children's needs, caring. Largely because the stereotypes and misunderstandings about fathers run so deep in our culture, it has taken us an inordinately long time to notice these simple facts of life. Even people who should have known better often did not. Anthropologist Margaret Mead was probably being ironic when she defined a father as a biological necessity before birth and a social accident after it, but she was also expressing a widely held view.

Fortunately, it is one that is beginning to change. Lately researchers have found that the sight of a newborn triggers the same repertoire of loving behaviors in a new father as it does in a new mother; he coos, stares at, and talks to his infant just as often and just as avidly. Until psychologist Ross Parke and his team began haunting the maternity ward of a small Wisconsin hospital several years ago, however, no one had ever noticed this. Dr. Parke did find that men are slightly slower to warm to their children—probably because they are not as biologically or culturally primed as women. But even this difference vanished when visiting times were adjusted to the fathers' schedules. Fathers kissed, hugged, rocked, touched and held their newborns just as much as their wives did.

The clinical name for this is "engrossment" and another group of investigators discovered that what produces it in women also produces it in men—early infant contact. In this report the sooner fathers were able to see their babies, the more absorbed and interested they were, and the more eager to touch, hold and play with their babies. If that early contact included being present at birth, they were also able to distinguish their child from other children (fathers absent from delivery did not report this) and felt more comfortable holding their infants.

Researchers found, however, that men played differently with their babies. Usually, they are more active and physical than mothers, but even this difference has its own part to play in the bonding drama since father–child interaction seems to make a woman more responsive. Dr. Parke and his colleagues noticed that when a father was present, his wife smiled more often at their baby and was more attentive to his needs. Because several other studies have uncovered similar behavior differences, many investigators now believe that each parent—by the way he or she relates to the child—makes a unique but complementary contribution to the infant's physical, emotional and intellectual development. Whether this is genetically or culturally determined is impossible to say. From the available evidence, I suspect social conditioning may play the larger role. Fathers and mothers act around their babies much like men and women are expected to act—in general. A woman almost invariably assumes a caretaker's role, more concerned with what are traditionally "womanly" duties: feeding, diapering and consoling the child. Fathers tend to be much more aggressive and playful with their children.

Probably the best example of the depth of these differences is a study done recently by a team of imaginative Boston researchers. Straightforward in design, it involved putting mothers, fathers and children together in a playroom and watching how they interacted. Within the sexes, the similarities were striking. Mothers, on the whole, were calm, protective and gentle with their children. Rarely did their interest flag or their tempers flare. Whether they were holding, hugging, talking or playing with their babies, they were almost always tender and calm. Fathers, in contrast, were much more excitable, mercurial, and rambunctious. Women talked more while men poked the baby gently with a finger or lifted him up in the air.

What is most striking about this study is the way each parent complements the other. But a child's self-confidence and self-image are the result of *all* the messages he receives from his parents. Whether this occurs through the stroking, hugging and gentleness of his mother or the physical play of his father, or vice versa, does not really matter. The important thing is that he receives jointly from his parents the encouragement to be himself.

As I said earlier, I suspect social conditioning determines who teaches what to the child. Dr. T. Berry Brazelton of Harvard has another, but not necessarily contradictory, explanation. "It seems to me," says Dr. Brazelton, "that the baby very carefully sets separate tracks for each parent—which, to me, means the baby wants different kinds of people as parents for his own needs. Perhaps the baby is bringing out the differences that are critical to him as well as to them."

The greatest mystery of all, though, is what accounts for father–infant attachment. Ultimately, it is love. But at the beginning the obvious psychological and physiological links that tie mother to child are lacking. Fathers do not carry children for nine months, never breastfeed them, only occasionally bottle-feed them, and rarely spend as much time with them as their wives do. Yet the bond that is eventually forged between them and their babies can be just as strong and vital as the mother–infant bond.

One way we have established this is by studying the child's mealtimes. Eating is as much an emotional act for an infant as it is a physical one. If he is uncomfortable or wary, he won't eat. Hence, if a baby drinks as much while his father is holding the bottle as he does when his mother is, that is a good indication he values both parents equally. This is what happened when a group of fathers and mothers were asked to feed their babies alternately. Milk consumption remained the same whichever parent was doing the feeding.

An even better measure of a baby's feelings toward his parents is to watch his reaction when one or the other of them leaves the room. "Separation-protest" is the rather heavy-handed name of this reaction, and over the years dozens of studies have been done using mothers; but until 1970, when an enterprising young investigator named Milton Kotelchuck organized what turned out to be his landmark study, no one had ever thought to include fathers. In design, the experiment was elegantly simple: Kotelchuck took 144 babies and measured their reactions when their mothers or fathers walked out of a playroom and left them alone with a stranger. He found that a father's leavetaking upset an infant as much as his mother's did. Many of the scientists present at the meeting where Kotelchuck read his paper were openly skeptical of his findings, reflecting our society's attitudes toward fathering. Yet this too is changing, as it must.

I would like to conclude this chapter with a letter that I received recently. It expresses better than all the research I have cited and the observations I have made what bonding is really about.

At the moment I saw you on TV I was holding and feeding my little three-month-old granddaughter, who is living here with us for a while, as her mother works. Her eyes were on me, and I felt a strong and very moving feeling of intimacy to her and from her and it is not something I can describe easily to you but it was very strong between her and me. I can't imagine that this feeling of intimacy will ever go away no matter how much time goes by. There was a contact between us, and I know she felt it inside of herself, without being able to put it into language. She let me know that she felt it, in her eyes.

Years ago, that same feeling came between her mother and me, when she was a little baby, and her mother and I feel it still, when we meet after a day's work, or even when we greet each other in the morning. "It"—whatever you can name it—is a bonding, a tie between our two souls, and it is most strong and lovely.

The contrast is the lack of it between my mother and me. I know that we were not bonded, for whatever reason I don't truly know, but we were never tied to each other like that. The wondering about what caused this gave much pain to my life, for I took it to mean for a long time that there had to be something wrong with me. I saw "it" between my friends and their mothers (in different degrees, but definitely more than what was between my mother and me) and this only made me feel more lonely.

Now I realize that "it" just did not happen, and my mind can rationalize it much better now. There was the war. I was born in February 1939. My mother saw my father enlist right away. Our father was never around those first months of life. He was in training for the Army. I don't have any memories of him at all until he returned from the war in late 1945. He was good to me, but distant. He was and is much more intimate to two more children born in the years after his return. I used to have to leave the house when I saw him cuddling and holding the little sister that came in 1954. I was 15 years old and I could feel the jealousy and the pain of it.

I am now 41, and I feel very little for my parents, in that "intimate" way. There is a respect for the physical caring of my life then, but there is nothing "else" between us. On the other hand those two children born in 1952 and 1954 feel a different thing entirely for them. There is a definite closeness there and I look at it, and I cannot believe sometimes that we have the same parents.

I cannot remember any memory of being as intimate with anyone, except my grandmother who loved me very much and I still remember it from her. I still remember how she smelt, all soapy and like lilacs. I remember her hair on my face and the feel of her skin, and her gentle Scottish accent. Even today when I hear that particular Northern Scot accent, tears come to my eyes. I cannot remember a moment of anything with her that wasn't warm and loving. It felt natural and normal to generate love towards her. It was almost magnetic. There was a "drawing" from her to me, and when my mother wasn't around or looking, I did everything I could to get close to my grandmother, to feel that "feeling" with her. And she always recognized it between us and took those few precious moments to give it importance. If she was washing my face, she'd linger for a moment to stroke my hair or tickle me or play a little game. My mother did everything she could to run down my grandmother, but she could not destroy that bond between us. Did it come in those first weeks of life? I've never thought of that until I started writing this to you. It might have come in those first weeks of life, when I was taken to her home.

A strange thing happened recently when we visited Toronto. My husband and I went to my grand-mother's grave for the first time, for she died while we were in British Columbia some years ago.

While we were looking for her grave, I heard in my mind a "lullabye"—I've heard bits of this song in my mind all my life, without ever knowing what it is—but it came on very strongly while I was searching for her grave. When I found her grave, I didn't want my husband near—and I felt embarrassed for feeling that way about him being there, for he had helped me find her grave all that morning. But it felt like I wanted to be alone with her, to plug into that special feeling we had shared together once again. I knew "she" wasn't in that grave at all—but I still felt these things towards her, and that song was so strongly there in my mind. I don't know what that "lullabye" means. It is very gentle music, very light and beautiful and it just filled that graveyard that day.

Until I met my husband, she was the only person I saw who loved me, *from her eyes!*

Hope this helps you.

Chapter Nine

The First Year

Within the past decade, the unthinking infant I learned about in medical school during the late 1950s has suddenly given way to an amazingly resilient, resourceful creature who emerges from the womb with what—to physicians of my generation—seems like a breathtaking array of emotional, intellectual and physical capacities. Far from being the insensate being depicted in our texts, this child can see, feel, touch, taste and play; he can respond, and be responded to, in complex ways; he even has demonstrable preferences in food, in games and conversation.

At birth and in the weeks immediately following it, he is not only aware, but already absorbing small amounts of visual stimulation. Push a toy toward or away from an infant, for instance, and he notices. Contrasts also catch his attention—in fact, his attraction for them is one of the reasons a mother may have trouble establishing direct eye contact. His gaze strays naturally to the exciting contrast provided by her hairline. This sometimes upsets a new mother who must chase her infant's eyes to establish direct eye contact.

Next to sight, sound is a newborn's principal tool for exploring his new world, and of all the sounds that fill it, the one uniquely suited to his hearing capabilities is the human voice. In talking to infants, adults instinctively raise their pitch and speak in five- to fifteen-second intervals; new tests show that this particular combination of timing and sound arouses and holds a newborn's very brief attention span better than any other.

Less is known about the infant's capacity for smell, though recent reports indicate there are at least four odors that make a strong impression on him. The first three are licorice, garlic and vinegar; the fourth is his mother—as Dr. Aidan Macfarlane demonstrated with a little help from some nursing mothers. As part of her experiment, Dr. Macfarlane asked the women to wear gauze pads inside their bras between feedings. Then she placed the worn pad on one side of each infant's head and a fresh, unworn one on the other side. If the infant turned to his mother's pad, Dr. Macfarlane reasoned, it meant he recognized her smell. In the tests, even five-day-olds showed a preference for the maternal pads.

Personality is much harder to measure, which may be why for generations conventional medical wisdom has held that a newborn did not have any. He was assumed to be a blank sheet whose personal style only begins to emerge when he has some life experience behind him. New research has challenged this view. Virtually all of the 141 infants examined in one study displayed vivid differences in style and temperament very soon after birth. Though the researchers did not explore where and how these differences originated, their report is worth examining because it is one of the few long-term personality studies ever done. During the ten years the youngsters were followed, the team made many insightful observations about the delicate interplay of heredity and environment in shaping personality. But some of their most exciting data were inspired by their subjects' behavior in early infancy.

At this stage, a newborn's reactions are blunt and one-dimensional, and can convey several different and contradictory meanings, which make it hard for an observer to know exactly what a baby is feeling because he may kick when he is happy, sad, frightened or anxious. Nevertheless, just the fact that he kicks a lot is significant, since a child's activity level is one of the first important indications of his future personality. Some infants move relatively little, and then only deliberately; others are constantly in motion. And while that kind of excessive activity does not always equate with high anxiety, the evidence suggests it is sometimes indicative of internal anxiety.

A boy the investigators called Donald is an eloquent case in point. "Donald," the team wrote, "exhibited an extremely high activity level almost from birth. At three months, his parents reported, 'he wiggled and moved about' while asleep. At six months, 'he swam like a fish during baths.' At 15 months, [they] found themselves 'always chasing after him.' " At three, he was still a study in constant motion. Even the enforced discipline of school could not slow him down. His kindergarten teacher reported, with humor and affection, that "he would hang on walls and climb on the ceiling." But a few years later his teachers were no longer finding his hyperactivity quite so endearing. The team observed that at age seven "Donald was encountering difficulty in school because he was unable to sit still long enough to learn anything and disturbed the other children by moving . . . about the classroom." Every superenergetic baby is not destined to grow into a Donald, of course. Activity is only one index of future personality. Furthermore, if a child's energy is properly channeled by his parents and teachers and he is allowed to express himself according to his own style, he may grow up into an active, happy and outgoing person.

A baby's reaction to change—new foods, people, places or routines—also reveals a great deal about him. By its nature, change is upsetting to all infants, but the doctors who conducted this study discovered that some babies, though momentarily thrown by it, settle down to a new routine or food easily. Others are a bit more difficult: They kick, scream, cry and generally cause a terrible and, for mothers, often unnerving ruckus. Age and experience do not always smooth away the edges of their anger, either. The investigators found that as one-, two- and three-year-olds, many of the excitable children in the study were overreacting to insignificant incidents, which suggests to me that they were really responding to earlier experiences at birth or in the womb.

Some of these early traits are only temporary expressions of a stage; they pass when the stage does. Others seem permanent, but because drives and desires that begin emerging in utero do not assume final form until the third or fourth year, they, too, are alterable. In fact, what happens in that intervening period is just as important in influencing their final shape as what happened in the womb.

As guide, companion and interpreter of the infant's new world, a parent not only helps determine his perception of that world but, to a significant extent, how successfully he functions in it. His intelligence, his language, his drives—all the skills he needs to master it—are significantly influenced by his mother and father and the quality of care they provide. The amount of attention (bonding) a baby receives even in the hours immediately after birth obviously makes an important difference in the kind of person he becomes. In the months that follow, his parents' responses—or lack of them—mark him in other crucial ways. Next to genetic inheritance, in fact, quality of parenting is the single most important factor in shaping the depth and breadth of intellect. What kinds of games a child is exposed to, the way he is addressed, and how he is treated all play a part in this process.

How these factors mesh with and influence the traits that have already begun forming in utero is still unclear largely because an abstraction like "self" is very difficult to define in a study. As we saw in Chapter 3, there is good reason to believe a rudimentary sense of self begins emerging in the womb. But unlike the fetus, the newborn* lives in an ever expanding little universe. Food, toys, noises, his mother exist only insofar as he can taste, touch, hear, feel or hold them. He does not yet know what people are, let alone how to act around them. Even a simple activity such as tickling, which Harvard psychiatrist Burton White has pointed out is a social as well as a physical phenomenon, is beyond him at this point. "To have a successful tickle," says Dr. White, "you have to

---

* The best single explanation of infant awareness—and the one that influenced my thinking most deeply—is Dr. Robert McCall's informative and thoughtful book *Infants: The New Knowledge.*

have a ticklee with a perception of a tickler nearby. You can tickle a two-month-old, but nothing will happen . . . a human being doesn't become ticklish until at least three and a half months old. It seems to be a sign of his growth of social awareness."

Perhaps one of the reasons that a two-month-old does not develop social awareness earlier is simple lack of time. In these early months, the infant is very busy exploring his environment and acquiring the skills he will need for learning later. At birth most of these skills—sight, hearing, taste, smell and feel, all essential learning tools—are already present and functioning. So, too, is memory. Considering all the practice he has had in utero, it is not surprising that a newborn excels in this area, as Dr. Steven Friedman demonstrated a few years ago. His subjects were only a few days old and obviously unable to tell him what they remembered; but a new object will attract even a very young baby's interest, so Dr. Friedman reasoned that if on the third or fourth appearance a checkerboard failed to stir his subjects' curiosity, it meant they remembered it. That is pretty much what happened. After several viewings the newborns turned away, bored, though they remembered the board's design well enough to respond when Dr. Friedman tried to outwit them—whenever a new board with a different number of checks was substituted, their interest quickly returned.

An infant, of course, can find more practical ways to use his memory, and he learns them quickly. Within a month or so, he is able to recall his mother's face, but since he is still looking largely at her eyes and forehead, the picture he carries of her probably bears a closer resemblance to one of Picasso's abstracts than to a human face. Another of the useful functions of memory is to remind him of his eating time. A few weeks are all he needs to learn his schedule and, according to a new report, he does not like unexpected alterations in it. In this study, babies used to feeding every three hours grew restless and uncomfortable if the interval stretched beyond that time. On the other hand, children, like adults, may get hungry before their appointed mealtime. The earlier we learn to respect the individual needs of the infant, the more we help him develop his self-esteem.

Perhaps the best measure of the infant's quickwittedness at this stage is his ability to mimic. Mimicry requires the mastery of many fairly sophisticated skills. First, the child has to understand that the adult making faces at him wants to be copied; second, he has to learn to copy these gestures; and third, he has to be enticed into this game by what is, for all intents and purposes, a purely abstract reward—the gratification of the person he is mimicking. For these reasons, until recently child psychologists believed that children younger than nine months old were incapable of it. But several new studies have demonstrated that even infants a few days old can mimic. In one landmark study, researchers had a nursery full of babies imitating them. Some of these babies were only one hour old! When a researcher stuck out his or her tongue, made a face, or wiggled fingers in front of a baby, the child often responded in kind. This (and other experiments like it) demonstrates conclusively the presence of well-developed (one could say adult) thinking, including the handling of abstract ideas, in the newborn.

Within a month or two, that infant can master even more sophisticated activities. I say "can" because several authorities, including Dr. Burton White of Harvard and

Dr. John Watson of the University of California, believe many infants fail to learn not because they are not bright enough or have not been shown, but because they have not been shown properly. Teaching a very young child is as much art as science. Parents can read all the right books, provide the right cues and still fail if they do not grasp a child's abilities and rhythms. Like the rest of us, infants learn best when what is being taught taps their natural abilities, and since a six- or seven-week-old is best at looking, grasping, sucking and vocalizing, the things he learns best and most quickly relate to these activities. Anything more complicated will not only elude him, but may harm him, particularly if it is pressed on him insistently by an overly ambitious parent.

Parents also sometimes forget that their child's response span at this stage isn't much greater than a long breath. Research has shown that the cues that encourage such actions as talking must be precisely timed. A child needs instant encouragement—meaning within five or six seconds—or he will not associate it with his behavior —which, in this case, means he will not feel encouraged to speak more.

Some of this is simply a matter of practice: As a parent gets to know the child's rhythms and reactions better, her or his own responses grow more finely tuned. Ideally, they should also grow more frequent. Isolating play and communication to thirty- or forty-five-minute daily intervals may be adequate (though in my opinion, just barely). But there is an almost geometric progression between the amount of meaningful time spent with a child and that child's intellectual and emotional growth, as was demonstrated a few years ago in the Harvard Pre-School Project, a unique and innovative early learning study headed by Dr. White. I will have more to say about it later, but one of the interesting things he and his colleagues found was that the usual indicators of a child's performance, such as parents' income, educational level and social standing, were far less important than quality of mothering. The brightest and most socially attractive infants and toddlers in the project came from diverse backgrounds, but all had mothers who were responsive, enthusiastic, communicative and generous with their time and emotions.

Child psychologist Mary Ainsworth of the University of Virginia calls such women "sensitive mothers." "A sensitive mother," she says, "is able to see things from her baby's point of view. She's tuned in to receive . . . [his] signals and . . . responds to them promptly and appropriately. Although she nearly always seems to give what he wants," Dr. Ainsworth says, even in refusing his wishes, "she tactfully acknowledges his signals and suggests suitable alternatives. She makes her responses . . . contingent . . . [on his] wishes and communications. By definition, she cannot be rejecting, interfering, or ignoring."

Of all the qualities that distinguish her from the insensitive mother, Dr. Ainsworth feels the most significant is her ability to empathize with her child and see the world from his perspective. "The insensitive mother," says the psychologist, "gears her interventions and initiations of action almost exclusively to her own wishes, moods and activities." By so doing she often either ignores or misinterprets her child's signals; either way the child suffers. Often an infant will lose faith in himself. Even a five- or six-week-old needs to feel his actions influence his surroundings. Each small success encourages him to try something a bit more ambitious and to feel secure in the knowledge that his wishes are being respected. Since, at this stage, he measures success in terms of his mother's responses, if she ignores or misinterprets his efforts, eventually he will give up trying. Psychologists call this "enforced helplessness," and you can see its effects in the three-year-old who does not know how to button his shirt, the seven-year-old who cannot tell time yet, and the thirty-year-old who believes his failures are due to circumstances beyond his control.

While the roots of this behavior may reach back to the womb, insensitivity toward the newborn in the first weeks of life can transform what was then only a tendency into a fixed trait that may seriously handicap a child just as he prepares for the next great leap in emotional and intellectual development, which occurs between the end of the second and the seventh month. For most of this period the very basic distinction between himself and the world continues to elude the infant; he remains, contentedly, the center of his own small universe. But having grown enormously both physically and intellectually, he is much better equipped to deal with the objective reality around him. He can see better now; in fact his vision is almost as good as an adult's. He is able to grasp, pick up, play with and discard larger, more complex objects. That has important consequences for his intellectual growth, since his new sophistication allows him to proceed from the very fundamental question "What is this?" to the more advanced one of "What can I do with this?"

Ideally, both the toys he is given and the games he plays at this stage should provide answers to that question. A ball is fine, but a ball that goes "thunk" or "bong" when it is squeezed or thrown is even better; a parent who goes "burp" when his ear is touched is infinitely more intriguing than one who simply smiles. This kind of play also contributes to a baby's sense of mastery. His touching and squeezing are making things happen, and his success in producing a change this time will encourage him to try something more adventurous next time. Perhaps this sense of mastery explains the popularity with infants of Dr. Stern's punch line game. Even in the role of audience, they get to feel they are affecting maternal behavior.

For all his newfound prowess, the three- or four-month-old is not yet ready to proceed beyond the basics. Balls, rattles and blocks are all he can handle now physically and emotionally and, because they exist only in relation to him, all are used in the same ways. Later, once he starts distinguishing between himself and the world, objects will take on an individual character and his play becomes tailored to the requirements of each particular toy. Balls will be thrown and squeezed more often than blocks, rattles will be shaken at least as often as they are chewed.

One of the few things a child does notice at this point is texture. Taste and touch—as well as looking and hearing—continue to be his primary ways of learning about the world. He will bite, chew, lick and look at almost anything, provided it has an interesting color, shape or smell. Properly directed, this rambunctious curiosity can even be turned into a form of play. A born natural at it, an infant does not need a great deal of supervision. Play is a good outlet for natural aggression. It is also an excellent way to broaden a child's intellectual horizons. Here are some examples of how:

- FEELING. Place him on different surfaces—a rug or blanket—so he can explore and feel textures.
- SEEING. Make a mobile by using colorful cardboard shapes to hang over his bed. He will enjoy watching the colors and shapes and soon start reaching for them.
- SMELLING. Put him in an infant seat while you are preparing lunch. Your presence will not only provide him with companionship, the kitchen will give him some new smells to discover.
- HEARING. Have a radio or record on while he is awake. The new sounds will stimulate him. (But the music should be relatively tranquil—no pounding rock. And do not let the radio become a substitute for your presence.)

Exercise is another activity that lends itself to learning. Babies love to move, and all their squirming, kicking and rocking provides them with useful information about the dimensions of their bodies and how each part works. To impose some discipline on these random movements in the form of exercise is to hasten the learning pace. To better acquaint a child with his arms, for instance, lay him down on his back and move one arm across his chest, then the other. Make the same movements with his legs. While he is lying on his back, offer him your fingers; then, once he has grasped them, gently raise him to a sitting position and slowly lower him down. A three- or four-month-old may still lack the strength for this game, but by the sixth or seventh month a child—girl or boy— should be able to keep a sturdy lock on parental fingers.

Though sex-related strength differences do not begin emerging until much later, at this stage boys and girls do begin acting in ways we think of as distinctly masculine and feminine. The first glimpse of what have been traditionally considered womanly qualities—empathy, responsiveness, emotionalism, altruism and sensitivity—are already on display in the nursery. Baby girls cry more than boys and they cry for what seem to be different reasons. Studies show girls are more likely to cry in response to another child's weeping. Girls smile more, and they respond differently to the human face. All babies like it, but girls seem to like it more. The sight of a face almost always sets off a stream of happy chatter in a female infant, while the male's response is less enthusiastic. In one study three-month-old girls much preferred looking at photos of faces to pictures of objects. Boys, on the other hand, were as content to look at pictures of one as of the other.

Though we do not know how many of these differences are produced by biology, recent research leaves little doubt that what may begin as meaningful, though minor constitutional differences, changes after years of social conditioning into major personality differences. One of the main reasons men and women act differently is that they have been taught to from infancy on. For example, a quality such as self-confidence, which is generally accepted by our society to be more of a male characteristic, is known to originate early and to be based on the amount of attention a person receives. So if men display it in greater numbers than females, it would seem that even as babies they were objects of more attention. That is exactly what studies show. Boy babies are talked to, cuddled and encouraged more than girls, and this difference continues through childhood and adolescence. Adventurousness is another largely male-stereotype trait that appears to stem, in part, from early learning. New research shows boy infants are given more freedom than girls to explore and get less supervision when they do.

What are generally regarded as typically male and female emotional characteristics also bear the heavy marks of early experience. If adult men are more restrained and controlled, and women more giving and responsive, is it any wonder, considering the way boy babies are taught to keep their feelings in check while girls are encouraged to express theirs? I don't think so. Nor do I think it is a good idea to continue perpetuating these learned differences. Social conditioning of this kind has needlessly and, sometimes, cruelly crushed the spirits of thousands of children.

Every child should be allowed to follow his or her own natural bent, and if that does not happen to fit a convenient social stereotype . . . then let us change the stereotype. The place to begin modifying our system, which is now heavily weighted toward male achievement and success, is in the nursery, where girls should receive the same encouragement, stimulation and attention as boys. Nowhere does this evenhandedness become more important than between the seventh and thirteenth months.

Early in this stage the child finally makes the crucial distinction between himself and the world. Babies start noticing that mothers, fathers, food, toys, sights and sounds lead an existence independent of them; this has important repercussions on their thinking. The single best illustration of the profound change in human intellect that occurs in this period is an experiment by Swiss psychologist Jean Piaget, conducted several decades ago.

Much of what we know about the growth of intellect we know because of the studies Piaget did of his own children's development. In this particular instance, he was trying to pinpoint exactly when people and objects begin taking on a separate life for the child; to that end, he devised a test, which he performed separately on his children when they were five or six months old.

In full view of each young Piaget, he took a toy and hid a portion of it under a coverlet. That posed no problem; as long as a portion showed the infant promptly crawled over and grabbed it. Then, adding an unexpected twist, Piaget covered all of the toy instead of just part. To retrieve it the child only had to crawl over and push off the cloth, which was still in full view. That one difference proved crucial. Though tested repeatedly, all the young Piagets lost interest in the hidden toy. They were still wrapped in their own world; once the toy disappeared from their view, it ceased to exist for them, just as parents and other objects did when they were not directly available to see or touch. Piaget conducted this experiment a second time when each of his children was a few months older. By this time they were able to grasp that the toy existed independently of them and, instead of losing interest in it after it was covered, they crawled over, pushed the cloth off, seized the toy and crawled away with it firmly in hand.

Behaviorally, this perceptual change produces a profound alteration in the child's relation to the people around him. Until now, he has not been terribly discriminating about the adults who pass through his world. Parents get bigger smiles than strangers and their departure upsets him more. But as Dr. Robert McCall, former Chairman of Psychology and Chief of Perceptual-Cognitive Development at Fels Research Institute, points out, what seems to matter most to the baby at five or four months is the presence of people rather than the presence of particular people. Strangers get big smiles and, left alone, a child of this age greets any new face almost as warmly as he would his mother's or father's. Around the seventh month (and in some youngsters, the sixth) this begins to change. He becomes wary if not downright suspicious; his entire countenance tightens now in the presence of a new person. The stranger is examined carefully and soberly and if he or she approaches the crib too fast or unexpectedly places a hand in it, a flood of tears is likely to follow.

Put this way, it sounds as if the child is reacting in fright and, considering the circumstances, that would be the logical explanation. Dr. McCall, however, thinks these confrontations produce the somewhat subtler feeling of uncertainty in the infant. As confounding an emotion as uncertainty is, even for an adult with all his years of social experience, imagine how troubling it is for an infant. Dr. McCall notes that if strangers represented an indiscriminate threat, their presence alone would cause alarm. But if approached slowly or engaged in a familiar game, an infant is usually fine. Coincidentally, both these behaviors also ease the anxiety produced by his uncertainty—the first by allowing the baby time to adjust to the new situation, the second by giving him something to do with the new person.

Since virtually all children between the ages of seven and twenty-four months react the same way to strangers, both behaviors should be incorporated into all introductions to a child. Give the baby a little time to examine a new person before bringing him or her over; if the infant is of speaking age, it is also a good idea to teach him some elementary social expression, such as "hi" and "bye-bye," which will give him something to do with the new person.

The child's new awareness causes some other problems as well. Now that he realizes his mother leads an independent existence, he no longer needs to wait helplessly for her to appear. The fact that she is summonable, combined with his new knowledge of things, provides the basis for a number of innovative and, I'm afraid, for mothers, sometimes exasperating games. One perennial favorite is "drop the toy." Whereas at an earlier age when it fell from sight he forgot about it and his mother could pick it up at her leisure, by this point he has not only discovered that dropping a toy is fun, but that this game can be played over and over again. All he needs is a toy that goes "bang" when it hits the floor and a willing mother to retrieve it.

Around this time he makes the somewhat more practical discovery that he can remember names for things. Simple words and his own name are recognizable to him, though he still cannot pronounce them. Next to the discovery of the world outside himself, this is the greatest intellectual breakthrough he makes in the first year. Language is the currency of all human knowledge, and even a silent grasp of it opens up new realms of learning. Expressions such as "mama," "papa," "hi" and "bye-bye" eventually lead to an understanding of rudimentary language and social skills.

Confirmation of this comes from the Harvard Pre-School Project, where infants and toddlers with the best grasp of language almost always scored highest in achievement tests. These scores are not that important since a child's test results often vary widely until his intelligence stabilizes around the age of three. But its basic foundations are laid in the years leading up to the third birthday, and, as I mentioned earlier, what distinguished the project's high scorers throughout their first years was quality of mothering. Emotional responsiveness was part of this, but their mothers were also intellectually responsive. They talked to their children: When handing over an object they pronounced its name; when they saw their children staring at something, they named it—every occasion became an opportunity for a conversation between mother and child. These women were not taught a special skill; they naturally enjoyed their children—being with them, showing them things, letting them roam freely about the house, exploring everything. From a very early age, their babies had become active, respected participants in family life with ready access to all family members at any time of the day or night. This rich social life was the second distinguishing characteristic of the project's brightest children.

One of the reasons these youngsters virtually could not fail was the number of supportive, nurturing adults their immediate environment provided as role models. A child naturally wants to be like the people he loves. So if he sees his father or mother enjoying reading, music or sports, he will try to develop an interest in those activities. There are, however, two important corollaries to this rule. A child should not be forced to do something simply because it is supposed to be good for him; and a parent should not pretend interests he or she does not really feel. Here are some other useful pointers about parenting to keep in mind:

- BE RESPECTFUL. Don't make the mistake of thinking that what you do or say around your child will not matter until he is two or three. As we have seen, it matters a great deal from pregnancy onward. A child is very perceptive and, if he senses he is not

being treated with respect, you may both end up
later paying for that.

- ENJOY YOUR YOUNGSTER. Don't try to raise a perfect
  child. You will only end up making everyone mis-
  erable. Despite claims to the contrary, there is also
  no such thing as a perfect child-rearing technique.
  While it is important to learn as much as you can
  from books, authorities and friends, in the end you
  have to be your own expert. Do what feels right to
  you and your partner and ignore the rest.
- DISCIPLINE. Too little is as bad as too much. Discipline should be moderate, appropriate and consis-
  tent. Don't punish a child for something you let him
  do the day before. If a behavior or activity is placed
  off-limits, it should remain off-limits. Don't be
  afraid to show your feelings. If your youngster has
  made you angry, let him know it firmly, but avoid
  screaming. Also be sure the anger is legitimate.
  Don't take out your frustrations on him.
- ENCOURAGE INTIMACY. Mothers generally need to be
  reminded of this less than fathers, especially fathers
  of sons. There is nothing unmanly about hugging,
  cuddling or kissing a son.
- BE YOUR OWN PERSON. Self-abnegation does not
  translate into good parenting. Your life and your
  marriage are important too. They should not suffer
  just because you have become a parent. Moreover,
  it is easier to be a good parent if you are fulfilled
  and secure yourself. Otherwise, there is the temptation to live vicariously through your child, and I
  can't think of a more certain prescription for dis-
  aster than that.

Chapter Ten

Retrieving Early Memories

According to traditional medical science, children prior to the age of two cannot remember anything because their large nerve tracts are not fully myelinized—that is, covered with a fatty sheath of connective tissue—and therefore cannot carry messages through them. This has been proved incorrect. The absence of myelin slows down conduction of nerve impulses but it does not prevent them from passing.

Traditional psychiatric opinion, for a different reason, also believed that children before two could not think. This was based on Freud's contention that only with the acquisition of language did children begin to use symbols and lay down memory engrams.

These traditionalists would probably dismiss such accounts as the following:

> When I was born in December 1960, my natural mother gave me up for adoption after giving me Il-

leen for a name. From there I was sent to another foster home, then was adopted at four months of age.

My adoptive parents chose to change my first name to Cheryl, as they felt it wouldn't matter at my young age. The strange thing is that when I came home from kindergarten one day I all of a sudden for no reason became very angry at my mother. She asked me what was wrong, and through my tears I told her I was mad because her and my father named me Cheryl. Trying to comfort me, she said they thought Cheryl was a nice name for a little girl, then she asked me what I would have rather been named. My answer was "Illeen! Illeen! I only like that name!" (She had never told me I was ever called Illeen.)

Yours very truly,
Mrs. Cheryl Young.

Or:

Dr. Thos. Verny,
In reply to your request on *Take 30* [a local television show] today I wish to let you know that I have memories prior to birth. I remember a feeling of warmth and comfort—I had a sense of hearing muffled sounds outside my environment and I could see a red hazy covering around me. I do not remember my birth (August 28th, 1913) but exactly 1 year later I remember being on a station platform in Creston, British Columbia (my birthplace) and seeing a trainload of soldiers with flags waving—going to the East. I have a photo (recently found) which proves this.

Yours truly,
Ron Gibbs

Today we know that from the sixth month of pregnancy onward and especially from the eighth month, memory templates are laid down that follow recognizable patterns. By then, the child's brain and nervous system are developed sufficiently to make this possible, and the fact that memories retrieved from this period have a recognizable shape and form tends to confirm the notion that the brain is operating near normal adult levels by the third trimester.

If our early recollections of prenatal events are such powerful shapers of behavior, why are we able to remember so few of them? New research has provided several possible answers to this question and it may well be that each separately, or, more likely, a combination of all, has an effect on memory.

Our inability to remember specific events or situations does not mean those experiences and the feelings that color them have been irretrievably lost. Even deeply buried memories remain emotionally resonant. One of the things that may cause them to slip from conscious recall, however, is a process involving oxytocin, which, as we have seen, is the hormone that controls the rate of labor contractions. Oxytocin, then, is essentially a muscle regulator, but one with a special effect. Recent research shows that in large quantities, oxytocin produces amnesia in laboratory animals; even thoroughly trained animals lose their ability to perform tasks under its influence. Why this is so is not entirely clear, but we do know a laboring woman's oxytocin floods her child's system. So if few of us are able to remember what happened at birth, it may be partly because—like those of the laboratory animals—our birth memories are washed away by the oxytocin we were exposed to during labor and delivery.

Our ability to retrieve them later may also be partly

dependent on another naturally occurring substance, ACTH (adrenocorticotropin hormone). New studies have shown that ACTH has the exact opposite effect of oxytocin—it helps retain memory, which would account for the many prenatal and birth memories that center around traumatic or disturbing events. When a pregnant or birthing woman is tense, pressured or fearful, her body responds by releasing stress hormones; the substance that regulates their flow is ACTH. The same thing happens when any of us becomes frightened or anxious. But in a pregnant woman, of course, it also acts on her child. Every time something frightens her, large amounts of the hormone flood into the child's system, helping him to retain a clear, vivid mental picture of her upset and its effect on him. This phenomenon could explain why, say, Ricky Burke, whom we met earlier, had such a graphic recollection of his birth. Ricky's mother was under terrible emotional stress the night he was born: She was dangerously early, in serious pain, and being treated in an emergency setting. The ACTH her body produced in response to these stresses probably contributed to her son's astonishing recall of the Latin prayer the priest had whispered over him and the angry words of his frustrated doctors.

This is in contrast to the circumstances in which the birth memory of one of my patients, whom I mentioned earlier, surfaced. She was the middle-aged woman who, in the middle of an exhausting session, suddenly had a vivid recollection of her mother's fear during birth. The fact that her mother was frightened—i.e., stressed—at that critical moment indicates ACTH helped produce the sharpness of her memory. Since her birth had been fairly routine, though, I suspect a phenomenon called "state-dependent learning" may also have aided memory retrieval.

Briefly, state-dependent learning refers to the fact that sometimes an event such as birth, which we experience in a state of physical and emotional arousal, becomes part of a mind-set comprising the memory of the event itself as well as the emotions and physical sensations attached to it. In such cases, we will often be unable to recall the event unless some other circumstance recreates the feelings that attended it. The power of this phenomenon has been demonstrated conclusively in laboratory studies. In one experiment, researchers used two very common feelings—fear and hunger—to turn memory on and off. A group of animals were frightened, then taught a particular set of tasks; as long as they were just frightened, they were able to remember how to perform those tasks perfectly. However, the addition of a second element—hunger—clouded their memories and, hence, their performance. Why the addition of a second element produces memory suppression we do not know. Nonetheless, this study does indicate that memory of a thing, person or event is influenced by the presence of a particular and very specific mind-set.

This phenomenon could easily explain why my patient's memory of her birth suddenly surfaced during that difficult session we had. In intense psychotherapy an individual is forced to work through a minefield of emotionally charged memories, and in the course of that hazardous journey, he or she may unwittingly—as my patient did—set off one of those mines. The person does not even have to be talking about a particular subject to retrieve spontaneously a memory related to it. My patient happened to be discussing her husband when the birth recollection surfaced. In state-dependent learning, what matters is not the circumstances, but the emotional or physiological "set" it produces. Something in our discussion of her husband—what, I have no idea—recreated the "set" this woman had experienced when her mother became fearful at her birth, and thus released a memory of that maternal fear.

The ability of certain pharmacological agents (drugs) to produce birth recollections may be due to the phenomenon of state-dependent learning. This was demonstrated in a classic experiment in which lab animals were injected with a drug and then taught to run a complicated maze of interlocking corridors. Whenever the animals were given the drug again, they moved through the maze like experienced travelers passing along a well-known route, but when a different agent was used, their knowledge of the maze fragmented. They were able to recall some of the routes, but not enough to bring them safely to the exit of the maze.

I think this finding explains why so many of the recollections that surface in memory experiments are birth related. Most of the subjects in those experiments were born at a time when medicated deliveries were standard. Evidently the agents they are given in the memory studies create a "set" similar to the one their birth medications produced. It may be that some of the substances used in these experiments chemically resemble the analgesics and sedatives used obstetrically twenty, thirty or forty years ago. Another possibility is that certain drugs may chemically or physiologically re-create the "set" a person experienced in utero or at birth, which would trigger an early memory.

This may have been why a patient I discussed earlier

was able to remember the sound of the carnival trumpets he had heard in utero only after taking a drug, and also why another patient remembered only while on medication the party incident at which his pregnant mother was humiliated. I strongly suspect in the latter case that ACTH may also have played an important role—first, because the situation the mother faced the night of the party was deeply stressful, so there must have been a large amount of ACTH in her system during and immediately after it; and second, because of the vividness of the impression. It seems to me that only a highly specific memory retrieval aid such as ACTH could produce such sharp prenatal recollections.

Psychiatrists and psychologists who regress patients regularly to birth and pre-birth times through drugs, hypnosis, free association or other means often report on experiences that appear to go back even as far as conception. Such accounts as the following are not uncommon:

"I am a sphere, a ball, a balloon, I am hollow, I have no arms, no legs, no teeth, I don't feel myself to have a front or back, up or down. I float, I fly, I spin. Sensations come from everywhere. It is as though I am a spherical eye."

Aside from the arresting imagery, there is not much in this description that seems to make sense—not in the way we expect memories to. But I have heard dozens of similar accounts from my own and other psychiatrists' patients and, more to the point, I have found that if you examine them closely, these recollections often correspond to events in the early stages of pregnancy. I cannot say that they represent bonafide prenatal memories; but given the internal logic they often display, I think it is a subject worth exploring in the future.

The fact that we do not consciously recall something does not mean that it was not recorded. This, by the way, also applies to people under a general anesthetic. With the help of hypnosis, people who are hypnotizable remember with great clarity everything that was said and done during their operations. Coming back then to the study of the memory of the unborn, we can safely deduce that certainly from the sixth month after conception his central nervous system is capable of receiving, processing and encoding messages. Neurological memory is most assuredly present at the beginning of the last trimester, when most babies, if born, can survive with the help of incubators.

Just as in the chapter on Intrauterine Bonding we had to postulate the existence of a third avenue of communication—i.e., sympathetic—in addition to the two physiological ones in order to account for all the observations, so here again we find ourselves in a parallel situation. For there are people, many thousands of them, who either through their dreams, their actions, their psychiatric symptoms or under other circumstances evidence "memories" that go back before the last trimester.

Evidence for some sort of an extraneurological memory system is growing. The fact that we possess such a faculty is further supported by well-documented cases of near-death experiences (see the writings of Kübler-Ross and others), where people who have been declared dead by their doctors return to life and report on every detail of what transpired in the room. They often know not only what was said but what was done to them, the expression on people's faces, what these people wore, and so on—things they could not have seen even if their eyes had been open—which they were not.

In the past the acquisition or expression of such knowledge has been called intuitive. Sympathetic communication between a mother and her unborn or the communication between any two people who have a very close emotional relationship, such as twins, are all good examples of intuition or extrasensory perception.

Since sympathetic messages, like messages along the central and autonomic nervous systems (CNS–ANS) must also lead somewhere and be encoded somewhere, I hypothesize that they are laid down in individual cells; I call memory so derived "organismic memory." This would allow even a single cell such as an ovum or a sperm to carry "memories," and would provide a physiological basis of explanation for the Jungian concept of the collective unconscious.

Consequently, what I am postulating are two separate but complementary systems serving our memory faculties. One depends for its functioning on the establishment of the mature neurological networks that comprise the CNS–ANS and is operative by the sixth month after conception. This system obeys the laws of physics and chemistry. The other is a para-neurological system. We are not as yet cognizant of the laws governing this system.

It seems to me that the sympathetic modality predominates at the beginning of one's life and then gradually diminishes. At times of great stress, such as for example danger to a loved one or imminent death, it reappears. It may also manifest itself in altered states of consciousness induced by, for example, hallucinogenic drugs, hypnosis or psychotherapy. For the time being I think that only by accepting this bi-polar model of memory, at least as a working hypothesis, can we explain not only the existence of prenatal and birth memories, but also the development of attitudinal predispositions and vulnerabilities in utero.

Chapter Eleven

Society and
the Unborn Child

Albert Einstein, preoccupied with the mysteries of relativity at his desk in the Swiss Patent Office, may have been practicing science at its purest, but he did not operate in a vacuum. His work was done within the confines of a tightly structured society and, like all major scientific discoveries, it proved to have important social, ethical, moral and legal consequences for that society. The same is true of the work of all great scientists: It changes the society in which it originates in fundamental ways. Almost certainly, the work of the men and women you have read about in this book will do the same.

How we view the fetus and the newborn and our thinking about how and when life originates, will be different because of them. And that is bound to raise some provocative legal and moral questions for all of us—whether we be physicians, lawyers, legislators or parents. Abortion is one obvious example. How should we view it in light of what we have learned recently about the fetus? The production of test-tube life is another. Is it wise, given what we now know about the unborn child's emotional needs? In this chapter, I would like to explore the ways in which the concepts and findings of pre- and perinatal psychology will influence our social institutions and our attitudes toward some of the issues raised here.

ABORTION

Strictly speaking, neither side in the abortion debate can draw much immediate support from the new discoveries of fetology and prenatal psychology. That debate is largely over the use of abortion in the first months of pregnancy, and most of our new discoveries focus on the fetus from the sixth month onward. But the abortion issue cannot be sidestepped, either, if for no other reason than that the thrust of our knowledge is moving steadily backward toward the origins of life.

A decade or two ago, the notion that a six-month-old fetus possessed consciousness would have been laughed at. Today, many consider it an accepted fact. A decade from now, as our techniques grow more sophisticated, that line could conceivably stand at three, perhaps even two months. Dr. Robert Rugg's and Dr. Landrum Shettles's *From Conception to Birth*, one of the best and most up-to-date source books on embryology, notes that "by the end of the first trimester the fetus has developed all of its major systems and is virtually a functioning organism," which means by the end of the third month the unborn child is fully formed; his arms, legs, eyes, ears, heart and blood vessels have, in miniature, assumed the shapes they will carry throughout life. Even more crucial, the first discernible signs of brain activity occur in this period.

Brain waves, which normally start in the eighth or ninth week (they have been detected as early as the fifth), quickly take on, in the words of one investigator, "a distinctly individual pattern." The same is true of body movements, which begin about this time. The first stirrings—usually slight changes in position—are discernible as early as the eighth week, but active movement does not usually start until the tenth or eleventh week. Thereafter, the child quickly masters a host of complex and increasingly individual movements; babies in utero have been photographed scratching their noses, sucking their thumbs, raising their heads and reaching out. Because a ten- or eleven-week-old child not only moves, but moves in a purposeful way, it raises the possibility that those faint EEG tracings—brain waves—in the second and third month are indicative of meaningful mental activity.

If the child were at the other end of life, that would be the interpretation. As Dr. Bernard Nathanson notes in his excellent book, *Aborting America,* the unborn child meets all the criteria for life established by the Harvard Medical School. Known simply as the Harvard Criteria, these were created in the late 1960s to help physicians redefine the line between life and death in light of new advances in medical technology. The four signs of death are: no response to external stimuli; no deep reflexes; no spontaneous movements or respiratory efforts; and no brain activity. These physiological guidelines are the best we can devise, since ego, spirit, self, soul—whatever name one chooses to define human life—lie well beyond our measurement tools. The fact that the unborn tests "alive" by all four criteria raises significant questions about our current attitudes toward abortion.

That is not to say that I oppose abortion. The loosening of legal restrictions on it in the early 1970s was unquestionably wise. I believe the choice to have or not to have a child should be left to the individual woman. It is her body and her mind and the final say in deciding how it is to be used should be hers. Moreover, forcing a reluctant mother-to-be to carry a child until term is ultimately self-defeating, since the experience is likely to end up damaging both her and the infant. Legalization has also taken abortion out of the back alleys and put it where it belongs, in the hands of medical professionals.

Nonetheless, I am disturbed by the way easy access to the procedure has affected some of our attitudes toward life. One measure of this is the large number of abortions performed for contraceptive reasons. This is often less a matter of carelessness than lack of education since most of the women who use the procedure to terminate unwanted pregnancies are either very young, very poor or both. More and better sex education in school, at home and in clinics could prevent many of these pregnancies in the first place. But because that education is often not available to those who need it most, studies indicate that a disturbingly large number of abortions are performed for contraceptive reasons. The figure Dr. Marlene Hunter arrived at after studying more than six hundred women who applied for abortions in one small community hospital was 70 percent. Psychiatrist Eloise Jones came up with a similar figure. Of the five hundred women she examined, 80 percent had not been using any means of contraception when they became pregnant.

Even more disturbing is the use of abortion as a means of sex selection. Thanks to recent technological break-throughs, we can now determine the sex of a child fairly early in pregnancy. According to what genetic counselors at several medical centers told the *Journal of the American Medical Association,* some couples have begun using this knowledge to pick the sex of their children (requesting an abortion if the fetus doesn't happen to be the "right" sex—usually male).

Fortunately, that attitude is still rare. I have done enough counseling to know abortion is a decision not made lightly by most women; it involves soul-searching and a great deal of pain. Everything family, friends, physician and community can do to ease that anguish should be done, but I also think a woman must be made fully aware that what is at stake is not a clump of inert cells but the beginnings of human life. The pro-abortion forces argue this biases counseling and is unfair. But unfair to whom? If a woman were undergoing a life-threatening operation, she would be thoroughly briefed about the dangers of the procedure. That informed consent is a right patients have fought for for more than a decade. Should informed consent not apply to abortions as well? If a doctor can spend several minutes explaining how he plans to remove a superfluous organ, such as the appendix, shouldn't he—shouldn't we—be willing to give this kind of decision equal time?

This is not to say there are no legitimate reasons for wanting an abortion. Nor does responsibility for overuse of the procedure lie solely with women. Men take little interest in and rarely hold themselves accountable for the results of their sexual activities. For the most part, men expect a woman to carry the responsibility for contraception, and, if need be, for abortion as well. Only when a man is married to or deeply involved with a woman is he usually willing to assume an active role in the abortion decision. That is not good enough.

The pro- and anti-abortion forces both offer counseling to women who must make the decision alone, but too often they are more interested in making converts than in dispensing objective advice. For balance, a woman could visit both, then make up her own mind. Ideally, the best source of support and guidance is a sensitive, understanding family physician, obstetrician, psychiatrist, or midwife. As you know, these are not easy to find.

Once having decided to go through with an abortion a woman should realize that the procedure is generally safe from major emotional and physical complications. In one recent American study, fewer than one in a thousand abortions produced serious emotional upset. An English report came up with an even lower figure, putting the incidence of a syndrome called post-abortion psychosis at 0.3 per thousand legal abortions. That is not only extraordinarily low in itself, it is also far lower than the incidence of post-delivery psychosis, which occurs 1.7 times per thousand births.

ASSEMBLY-LINE BABIES

The artificial insemination of a surrogate mother is an option that has recently become available to childless couples in which the wife is sterile. At a cost of up to twenty thousand dollars Dr. Richard Levin, who heads Louisville's Surrogate Parenting Association, will arrange for a woman to be impregnated by the husband (via sperm transfer), carry the resulting child to term, and sign it over to the couple at birth. The first such child was born in November 1980. Undoubtedly, many more will follow in the coming years.

Medically, all the problems have been worked out; sperm transfer is simple, inexpensive and safe. Legally, however, it raises some knotty questions. First and foremost, it is unclear to whom the child belongs: the couple or the husband and the surrogate mother. The existing contracts require the child to be surrendered to the couple for adoption, but many legal authorities believe the courts would not take a child away from its natural mother no matter what the contract stipulates. Angela Holder, director of Yale University's program in law, science and medicine, says "there's not a court in the United States that would uphold such a contract if the surrogate mother wanted to keep the child." George Annas, professor of Law and Medicine at Boston University, is equally sure a couple who decided not to take delivery of their baby because it was deformed, retarded or for any other reason could break their contract as easily.

Even if these legal tangles could be resolved, is the use of a surrogate mother wise? True, it provides a childless couple with an infant that is, biologically, at least half theirs, and I can understand how some couples might prefer this option to adoption. At the very least, though, one has to question the motives of the woman who chooses to become a surrogate. Does she do it because she enjoys being pregnant or strictly for the money? The answer in most cases, I suspect, is for the money. A surrogate mother would naturally resist becoming emotionally involved with the child she is carrying. If she did not, giving him up later would be too painful. What kind of sacrifices would such a mother make for her infant? Would she stop smoking and drinking and be careful about what she eats? In labor would she hold out for a natural, though perhaps more painful delivery, or take the easy way out in the form of analgesics and anesthetics regardless of their effect on the infant? And, in the circumstances, would she allow herself to love or respect the life within her?

No doubt, defenders of the practice would argue that careful screening and monitoring of surrogate candidates could eliminate these dangers. Perhaps they could, but until that has been demonstrated in a scientific manner, I think some safeguards should be imposed on this phenomenon.

Similar questions are raised by a second recent development, "test-tube" babies. Louise Brown was the first child to begin her life this way, with the help of Drs. Patrick C. Steptoe and Robert Edwards and their colleagues at the University of London. Although Louise was born only a few years ago, advances in this area have been so rapid, there are likely to be thousands of other such test-tube babies by the end of the 1980s. Medically, the procedure is simple to administer. It involves the surgical removal of the mature human egg cells from the mother's body, which are then fertilized by the father's sperm in a test tube; when fertilization occurs, implantation is made in the mother-to-be. Thus, for all intents and purposes, the child grows to maturity in a normal uterine environment, which seems to make this procedure the ideal answer to one of the major causes of female infertility (diseased or abnormally shaped Fallopian tubes). And in many ways it is; the woman not only becomes pregnant by her husband, she is also able to carry the baby through pregnancy. In exchange, the baby is nestled in a warm, loving mother who, given her history, is likely to do everything possible for his well-being.

Laudable as all this is, there are some things about it that trouble me deeply. The manufacturing of life represents a massive intervention against nature and, if our past experience is any guide, hazards we do not even know enough to anticipate await us. This is often less the fault of the intervention than the way it ends up being used. Given medicine's predilection for mechanical and biological tinkering, will it be able to resist the temptation to employ this technique on a wholesale basis? The history of fetal monitoring is hardly encouraging on this score. Designed specifically for high-risk infants, the application of monitoring to all births has produced a sharp increase in the Caesarean rate. The use of induced labor, forceps and incubators has also increased needlessly. Test-tube baby production may follow the same course. And because it represents an intervention of immense proportions, its potential for harm is all that much greater. How do we know, for instance, that the genes carried in a fertilized ovum will not be irrevocably damaged in the process of transfer? Until we learn as much about its hazards as we do about its advantages, this technique should not be used on a wide scale.

OBSTETRICS

Not long ago, Dr. John B. Franklin, medical director of the Booth Maternity Center in Philadelphia, described the care and treatment of the healthy pregnant woman as "the great battleground" in obstetrics today. "Do we treat her as sick until proven well," he asked, or "well until proven sick?" In too many instances, he said, she is treated "sick until proven well." As I have pointed out previously, thousands of perfectly healthy women and infants have been needlessly endangered because of this attitude. Not everyone admitted to the obstetrical floor has to be medicated, monitored or operated on, and I think a growing number of obstetricians are finally beginning to grasp this fact. Nudged by their patients and their own sense of what is medically right, many have started scaling down the technological aspects of their practice—reserving them for cases of real need. In large metropolitan centers there is, in fact, a growing sense of change within the specialty these days. It is apparent in the way obstetricians talk and in their greater willingness to participate in natural births, to work alongside midwives, and to conduct deliveries in alternative birthing centers and other non-medical settings.

Encouraging as this is, it still is not enough. If we are truly to maximize the pregnancy and birth experiences, we also need a new kind of prenatal care—one that stresses the dignity, humanness and naturalness of these events, that puts as much emphasis on a woman's psychological needs as it does on her physical ones, and allows her and her family a voice in *all* decisions. Specifically, what we need is a comprehensive plan of care (preferably available under one roof, such as a medical center or special clinic) that treats the total woman by providing her with a wide array of medical, psychological and social support services. Among them:

- A Birth Counselor. As an experienced sympathetic advisor, the counselor, who could be either a doctor or midwife, would help the woman plan her pregnancy and birth goals. He or she would also aid in implementing those goals by directing the woman to the professionals and institutions that provide the kind of care she wants.

- MEDICAL SERVICES. Included here would be such routine kinds of care as periodic physical examinations and laboratory tests, as well as special services for the high-risk mother and genetic counseling.
- PRENATAL CLASSES. These would instruct participants in sex and nutrition education, in the anatomy and physiology of birth, and teach breathing and relaxation exercises.
- PSYCHOLOGICAL COUNSELING. An umbrella service, this would offer therapy for those with special problems, such as single mothers and couples having difficulty adjusting to pregnancy; but its centerpiece, a psychological screening test, would be administered to *all* pregnant women. Already used highly successfully in Sweden, West Germany and several other European countries to spot emotionally high-risk women, these tests contain questions built around potentially telling areas of emotional vulnerability, such as a woman's relationship with her mother, her self-image, her feelings and fears about delivery, her relationship with husband and father, and her psychiatric history.

The great value of these services is that they function as a kind of early warning system. The psychological test, for example, should be given during the first or second prenatal visit; if an expectant mother scores highly in one or several areas, there is still plenty of time to intervene with corrective measures. Normally, the nature of the measures will be determined by the woman's emotional vulnerabilities, but almost always some form of psychological therapy is involved. It might be marriage counseling, if the problem is a strained marital relationship, or group therapy with other expectant mothers if the fears center on pregnancy.

A less obvious advantage of these tests is that they would encourage obstetricians and psychiatrists to work more closely together, which would benefit them as well as the mothers and their children.

PSYCHIATRY

At the moment, obstetricians and psychiatrists are like two distantly related members of the same family. Contact between them is polite but infrequent, and mostly limited to an exchange of information about patients they have in common. The fact that they might share mutual interests and skills that fuse at a critical juncture in the human experience has not been sufficiently appreciated by most members of either profession. Obstetricians have been content to work their side of the fence unaided and, normally, the only time a psychiatrist sees the inside of an obstetrical ward after internship is when his own children are born or he is called on to treat a woman suffering from post-partum depression. This attitude has to change and if the first step in changing it is the development of a more psychologically oriented obstetrics, the second would be the emergence of a more obstetrically inclined psychiatry.

Flip through any psychiatric journal at random and you will find studies on new tranquilizers, antidepressants, electro-convulsive treatment, and behavior therapy for schizophrenics. But rarely in these journals will you see anyone addressing him- or herself to the effects of pregnancy-induced stresses and anxieties, and never to the psyche of the unborn child. Yet, the active involvement of psychiatry in obstetrics-related emotional issues could benefit thousands of women and their children. Attention and research should be focused on such problems as the high-risk expectant mother. We have already spotted her in three guises: the woman who worries inordinately about her body image, the one who has a bad relationship with her own mother and the one who has troubles with her husband. She probably comes in several other guises as well. One logical candidate for examination is the pregnant family breadwinner. Another is the woman who is forced to uproot herself and move during pregnancy. Evidence indicates a woman's attitudes toward birth predetermine the kind of delivery she has, but we need to know more about these attitudes so they can be spotted quickly and treated.

Psychiatry should also provide a program of short-term, problem-oriented therapy during pregnancy. Every woman who has seen her body change, who worries how that will affect her husband's feelings, who has nightmares about bearing a deformed or retarded child, or who is concerned about her adequacy as a mother, is experiencing pregnancy-related stress. These anxieties are common and often harmless, but they come dangerously close to unhinging some women. These expectant mothers are not necessarily weaker than other women, nor should they think of themselves as such. In my own experience, their most common problem is the lack of a support system in the form of a husband, friends or family to share their fears with. Unspoken fears grow larger as time passes. Often, the only real treatment these women need is a chance to talk with someone. Their concerns can usually be resolved in a few sessions with a sympathetic professional counselor. The added pressures of pregnancy can be deeply unsettling to an expectant father as well. Many of them may also benefit from a few visits to a psychotherapist.

This happens now infrequently and haphazardly; an enlightened obstetrician notices what he thinks is a troubled patient and refers her for psychiatric evaluation, or a psychiatrist finds that one of his recently pregnant "regulars" isn't adjusting well to her new condition and inquires further about it. What I am proposing is something far more sweeping: a structured system that would include a referral mechanism similar to the one obstetricians and pediatricians employ, and a course of psychiatric care designed specifically around the pregnant woman and her problems.

This and the other suggestions I have made so far are not difficult to implement. But if we are to make psychiatry truly responsive and effective, the discoveries of prenatal psychology and fetology will also have to be integrated into its treatment of childhood and adult emotional disorders, and that will involve some fundamental and, perhaps, painful changes for psychiatrists.

Fortunately, a survey I conducted among my colleagues in the Ontario Psychiatric Association reveals a surprising and encouraging receptivity to many of the ideas advanced in this book. Whether it is because of their own personal experiences in dealing with spontaneous prenatal and birth memories or their awareness of recent research I do not know, but more than half the survey respondents felt birth experiences influence personality; three quarters were sure memories begin to develop before the age of two; and a significant number were convinced that memories form before birth as well. This last finding shows that the discoveries of prenatal psychology are reaching my colleagues. It may seem incongruous that many of these same respondents also confessed they had not yet translated this new awareness into their work with patients. Partly this is due to the difficulty of changing ingrained habits, and partly to technical problems—a way has to be found to incorporate any discovery into a realistic mode of treatment.

In the case of prenatal psychology, this process is only just beginning, but the few innovative techniques that it has spawned are already showing enormous promise. The setting for one of the most promising of these is the charming seaside village of Cagnes-sur-Mer, a few miles west of Nice on the French Riviera. There, disturbed children from all over Europe are brought for treatment at an unusual clinic created by otolaryngologist Alfred Tomatis.

Otolaryngology is a rather unusual specialty for a man deeply interested in the birth experience. But it was Dr. Tomatis's work with the speech and hearing problems of troubled youngsters that led to his interest in the subject. Observing the behavior of his young patients, Dr. Tomatis came to two important conclusions: First, hearing and emotion are seated in the same area of the brain; and second, because of that proximity, hearing disorders are often a reflection of emotional difficulties produced by pregnancy or birth traumas. To treat the first effectively, Dr. Tomatis concluded, it was necessary to begin by treating the second; this led to the establishment of his clinic in Paris as well as others in western Europe and

Canada. The clinics' patients range in age from one month to twelve years,* and suffer from a wide range of emotional problems; but in one respect, nearly all are alike. They are victims of traumatic pregnancies or deliveries.

During a visit to Cagnes-sur-Mer in 1980, I was struck by how scrupulously the clinic's staff had re-created the womb and birth experiences. The centerpiece of the program is a tiny, egg-shaped room where each child undergoes several "rebirthing" or "reparenting" sessions. Everything about this unique space is designed to reproduce warm, reassuring, womblike feelings. Before entering, a youngster is massaged with coconut oil, and while in the room, he sits in a bath heated to the temperature of amniotic fluid. Meanwhile, he and the room are bathed in ultraviolet light that simulates the light an unborn sees when his mother is sunbathing (and which can be adjusted for a child's particular problem—a tranquil blue if he is hyperactive, an exciting red if he is apathetic).

Sound is another important feature of these sessions. The recording of his mother's voice, which is piped into the room during each session, is initially distorted to duplicate the way her voice sounds in the womb. But as treatment progresses, the distortion is gradually lessened until the child hears her normal speaking voice. Immediately after each session, the youngster is taken to the clinic's playroom, which overlooks a lovely garden, and urged to play, paint or sculpt. This part of the treatment is designed to help the patient relive and express old traumas.

* Dr. Tomatis also treats disturbed adults at his Paris center.

The clinic's director, child psychologist Ann Marie Saurel, told me that 70 percent of her young patients leave the clinic cured or improved. And to illustrate the point she told me about a sixteen-month-old named Claude who came to her with a head spasm that kept his head pinned to his left shoulder and with such severe limitations in the movement of his left arm he could hardly crawl. He would shrink from any bodily contact with his mother, who was as distraught by this as she was by his physical handicap. A careful history of the child revealed that during the eighth month of her pregnancy his mother had undergone amniocentesis during which the needle unfortunately nicked Claude's neck on the left side. That explained the protective attitude he had adopted to that part of the body as well as a severe distrust of his mother. This child totally recovered after six months of treatment at the clinic. Dr. Tomatis's therapy represents the only treatment modality I know of that can help children suffering from psychological problems through non-verbal methods, which in my opinion makes it a unique advance on present therapeutic approaches.

Isolation tanks for adults, which have become popular in several parts of the United States recently, bear a superficial resemblance to Dr. Tomatis's rebirthing pool. Filled with warm water and Epsom salts, these are supposed to create a womblike atmosphere for clients who pay fifteen dollars and upward for the privilege of floating inside one for an hour. I have no doubt they are a pleasant place to relax. Their resemblance to a legitimate medical technique is purely coincidental, though.

PEDIATRICS

Technologically, pediatrics, like obstetrics, has advanced light-years in the past few decades. That technology now routinely saves premature and sick infants who would have been lost only a few years ago. At the same time, it has created a dilemma for the specialty, which, in many ways, is as painful as the one obstetricians face. The inception of Neonate Intensive Care Units (NICUs) has created its own special hazards. Studies show that while in isolation a child is likely to grow more slowly, but those dangers pale in comparison to the alienation that enforced separation sometimes produces in parents and children. As I pointed out earlier, disruption of the bonding mechanism can influence a woman's attitude toward her child, and isolation in an NICU represents a massive disruption. Little wonder that child abuse and, according to data from Russia, the rate of children put up for adoption, are significantly higher for premature infants than for full-term babies.

Since these problems clearly grow out of the NICU-imposed separation of mother and child, the obvious solution is to open the units to parents for regular visits. All the available evidence indicates that mothers and infants would do better then. As I mentioned earlier, one recent study, in fact, found that premature babies who had been visited and touched regularly had significantly higher IQs than youngsters kept in isolation. Furthermore, there is no medical justification for isolation. When Stanford University's NICU was opened to parents, pediatricians at the facility expected an increase in the unit's infection rate; it never materialized. In fact, according to the investigators who were studying the effect of the liberalized visiting policy, the most diligent, meticulous scrubbers entering the NICU were the infants' mothers —which stands to reason, since their children were the ones at risk.

Far too many of the health professionals who run these units still place priority on efficient administration rather than on the emotional health of their patients. According to one recent study, only a third of the NICUs in the United States currently welcome parents. Unfortunately, the child of a young mother I learned about recently was not in one of those friendly units. Born more than two months prematurely, he was rushed immediately to an NICU and remained isolated in it for several weeks while he hovered between life and death. For most of that time, his mother sat quietly in the unit's reception area. When she was finally able to take her child home, it took her weeks to learn to treat him as if he were a "normal" baby. There is no need for this. Parents can be and should insist on being involved in the care of their premature babies even if they are in NICUs. Hopefully, the trend toward greater participation of the mother in the care of her premature infant even when he is in an incubator or respirator will be supported by pediatricians, neonatologists and others involved in the management of prematures.

However, an expectant mother should always keep in mind that she may require a Caesarean section and/or have a premature child. Therefore, in addition to arranging the type of delivery she desires, she should also make certain that the intensive care unit to which her premature baby would be taken is one with a liberal pol-

icy on visiting and relating to the infant. If such a precau-
tion is not taken prior to delivery, the mother may be in
no position later to gain access to her premature baby.
My comments about premature babies apply equally to
sick babies, in the sense that no effort should be spared
to provide many opportunities for both parents to inter-
act with the sick child in order to further the development of parent–infant attachment and to benefit the
physical and emotional needs of the child as well as the
parents.

Dr. Justin C. Call, professor and Chief of Infant, Child
and Adolescent Psychiatry at the University of California
at Irvine, says that by the age of six months, an infant is
capable of feeling depression in response to a loss such
as permanent separation from his mother; I of course
concur with that. The infant expresses his depression in
sleep disorders; gastrointestinal upsets such as refusal to
eat, vomiting and diarrhea; and withdrawal from people.
It is my hope that more pediatricians and child psychiatrists will recognize such symptoms as signs of an emotional problem and treat the child accordingly.

Some behavioral problems are predictable prenatally
and may appear immediately upon birth, as is the case
with babies whose mothers are alcoholics or drug addicts.
Similarly, babies whose mothers have undergone severe
stress, as I described in some of the previous chapters,
should receive special attention in the early postnatal
period. Any baby that withdraws from being held, that
constantly cries, that fails to gain weight may be
communicating through these ways his emotional
distress.

Hyperactivity often begins in the womb, and the
mother of such a child may report that he was a "whirling

dervish" before birth, never giving her a moment's rest. "If this activity pattern is not recognized and dealt with," according to Dr. Reginald S. Lourie, chairman of the School of Medicine at Irvine, "both the child and the parents suffer. An infant unable to put the brakes on his own racing motor feels helpless and out of control. Meanwhile, his parents are distraught that they can't calm him down." Instead of giving the child and the mother tranquilizers, clinicians need to *talk* to the mother and help her understand and cope with the special needs of this particular child, while at the same time reassuring her that the problem is temporary and treatable.

At the beginning of this book I cited research on the effect of playing a tape of maternal heart sounds to a group of newborns in a hospital nursery. As you will remember, the group that was exposed to the maternal heart sounds gained more weight and slept more (which are obviously interrelated) than a control group. Is there any reason why such a simple procedure could not be universally adopted?

Dr. Michele Clements at the City of London Maternity Hospital reported a baby who, after a difficult birth, in spite of all standard medical attempts at reviving him, would not breathe. She switched on in desperation her "womb music" tape, which she happened to have nearby, and the baby miraculously gasped and began to breathe.

This same tape, produced commercially by a Japanese scientist, is also utilized by Dr. Clements to test the newborn's hearing. Based on what we now know about the importance of bonding and the role that the mother's voice plays in this process, it is obviously essential for the well-being of the infant to recognize any hearing problems he may have. The same applies to visual deficiencies. At this time hardly anyone checks a baby's hearing and vision until very severe problems develop at about eighteen months or later. Although this is not in itself a psychological problem, it obviously can very rapidly influence the way the infant perceives his world, the way he reacts to it or fails to react to it, with consequent negative changes in the attitudes of the parents and caretakers toward the child. If the baby does not look at you or does not turn toward you when you speak to him, you will begin to think of him as strange, withdrawn, difficult, and so on, and begin to treat him differently. In the long run this will become a self-fulfilling prophecy; the child who started with a physical problem will also end up with an emotional one. This is an area that requires the close cooperation of pediatricians, child psychiatrists, audiologists and very observant parents.

If you as a parent suspect that your baby may have the slightest problem—talk to your doctor. I know so many mothers and fathers who don't want to "bother" the doctor with "imagined fears." Well, bother him or her. That is the doctor's job and he or she is well paid for it. When it comes to the health of your child, be like a dragon and not a mouse.

PREGNANCY AND WORK

Work has become a fact of life for millions of women, but unlike their male colleagues in offices and factories, they are often saddled with the competing demands of motherhood and employment. While most women juggle the responsibilities of both with admirable dexterity, our new awareness of the infant's and unborn child's sensitivities and capabilities adds an extra dimension to those responsibilities; the last three months of pregnancy and the first year after birth represent for the child a period of rapid learning. As the psychological and emotional imperatives that will rule his life begin forming, he needs her attention, support and nurturing. The best way of providing those is an extended pregnancy leave that covers the last trimester (a woman working in a noisy or high anxiety atmosphere should stop as soon as possible) and the first year after birth. I realize this is a great deal of time, and many women, for financial or other reasons, will not be able to comply. In those instances, every effort should be made to provide in quality what is lost in quantity of time. A judicious and thoughtful use of nights and weekends can go a long way toward meeting a child's needs. A growing number of fathers are also beginning to take time off during the first years. I see every reason, in the light of what we have said so far, for this trend to continue.

The paramount concern—for parents, for physicians, for educators, for all of us—should be the raising of a healthy child. Our collective hopes, dreams and wisdom reside with him; he is our future, and if it is to be a future free of the ugly turmoil and needless suffering that have so often marred our past, that child must be treated with the love and respect a human being deserves.

Notes

CHAPTER 1
The Secret Life of the Unborn Child

p. 19

Conditioned learning. D.K. Spelt, "The Conditioning of the Human Fetus in Utero," *Journal of Experimental Psychology*, 38:338–346, 1948.

p. 20

Smoking. Michael Lieberman, "Smoking and the Fetus," *American Journal of Obstetrics*, August 5, 1970.

p. 25

Anxiety. Lester W. Sontag, "Somatophysics of Personality and Body Function," *Vita Humana*, pp. 1–10, November 1963.

p. 27

Schizophrenic mothers. There are a number of excellent studies on this subject, among them Melvin Zax *et al.*, "Birth Outcomes in the Offspring of Mentally Disordered Women," *American Journal of Orthopsychiatry*, pp. 218–230, April 1977. See also Zax *et al.*, "Perinatal Characteristics in the Offspring of Schizophrenic Women," *Journal of Nervous and Mental Diseases*, 157:191–199, 1973.

p. 28

Maternal heartbeat. Lee Salk, "The Effects of Normal Heartbeat Sound on the Behavior of the Newborn Infant: Implications for Mental Health," from a paper delivered at the World Federation of Mental Health in Edinburgh, 1960.

p. 30

Father bonding. Gail Peterson *et al.,* "The Role of Some Birth-Related Variables in Father Attachment," *American Journal of Orthopsychiatry,* 49 (2):330–338, April 1979.

CHAPTER 2
The New Knowledge

p. 32

Autistic child. Personal communication from Dr. Alfred Tomatis to author.

p. 33

Prenatal clinics. Antonio J. Ferreira, "Emotional Factors in Prenatal Environment," *The Journal of Nervous and Mental Disease,* 141:108–117, 1965. This is the best short history of prenatal influence I know of. See also Ashley Montagu, *Prenatal Influences* (Charles C. Thomas, Springfield, Ill., 1962), p. 169.

pp. 36–37

Reflexes, facial movements. Maria Z. Salam and Raymond D. Adams, "New Horizons in the Neurology of Childhood," *Perspectives in Biology and Medicine,* Spring 1966, pp. 384–410.

p. 37

Baby sleeping, fetal reactions to cold, sweets and tickling. Albert Liley, "The Fetus as a Personality," *The Australian and New Zealand Journal of Psychiatry,* 6:99–105, 1972. A delightful and highly readable account of fetal idiosyncrasies.

p. 38

Fetal hearing. Erik Wedenberg and Bjorn Johansson, "When the Fetus Isn't Listening," *Medical World News,* pp. 28–29, April 1970.

p. 38

Maternal heartbeat, metronome, drum rhythms. Liley, *op cit.,* p. 104.

p. 39

Musical tastes. Michele Clements, "Observations on Certain Aspects of Neonatal Behavior in Response to Auditory Stimuli," paper presented at 5th International Congress of Psychosomatic Obstetrics and Gynecology, Rome, 1977.

p. 40

Fetal reactions to light. Liley, *op cit.,* p. 103.

Vision at birth. Robert McCall, *Infants: The New Knowledge* (Harvard University Press, Cambridge, Mass., 1979), p. 51.

p. 41

Consciousness. Dominick Purpura, *Behavior Today.* June 2, 1975, p. 494.

p. 42

REM Waves. Salam and Adams, *op cit.,* p. 387.

Brain exercises. H.P. Roffwaag *et al.* in McCall, *op cit.,* p. 48.

Prenatal memory. Stanislav Grof, *Realms of the Human Unconscious* (E.P. Dutton, New York, 1976), p. 161.

p. 43

Fetal catecholamines. Frederick Kruse, "Nos Souvenirs du Corps Maternel," *Psychologie Heute,* p. 56, June 25, 1978.

p. 45

Effects of different stresses. Dennis Stott, "Follow-up Study from Birth of the Effects of Prenatal Stresses," *Developmental Medicine and Child Neurology,* 15:770–787, 1973.

p. 47

Maternal attitudes. Monika Lukesch, "Psychologie Faktoren der Schwangerschaft," dissertation, University of Salzburg, 1975.

p. 48

Reading maternal stresses. Gerhard Rottman. "Untersuchungen uber Einstellung zur Schwangerschaft und zur fotalen Entwiklung," *Geist und Psyche,* Hans Graber, editor (Kindler Verlag, München, 1974).

p. 49

Effect of husbands. Dennis Stott, "Children in the Womb: The Effects of Stress," *New Society,* pp. 329–331, May 19, 1977.

p. 51

Personality styles. Sontag, *op cit.*, p. 1.

CHAPTER 3
The Prenatal Self

p. 53

Generation of war babies. Lester W. Sontag, "War and the Fetal Maternal Relationship," *Marriage and Family Living*, 6:1–5, 1944.

p. 54

Predisposition toward emotional disorder, Sontag, "Somatophysics," *op cit.*, p. 2.

p. 56

Famine and hypothalamic vulnerability. G.P. Ravelli *et al.*, "Obesity in Young Men after Famine Exposure in Utero and Early Infancy," *The New England Journal of Medicine*, August 12, 1976, pp. 349–353.

p. 57

Father's death and hypothalamic vulnerability. Matti O. Huttunen and Pekka Niskanen, "Prenatal Loss of Father and Psychiatric Disorders," *Archives of General Psychiatry*, pp. 429–431, April 1978.

p. 58

Hyperactive ANS. Lester W. Sontag, "Significance of Fetal Environmental Differences," *American Journal of Obstetrics & Gynecology*, 42:996–1003, 1941.

Neurotic infant. Sontag in Ashley Montagu, *Life before Birth* (New American Library, New York, 1964), p. 50.

p. 59

Reading difficulties. R. Davis *et al.*, *From Birth to Seven: The Second Report of the National Child Development Study* (Longmans Group, London, 1972).

p. 60

Progesterone and estrogen study. "Prenatal Hormones Change Style of Play," *Medical World News*, pp. 35–36, March 31, 1980.

p. 65

Seeing and vision. Lietaert Peerbolte from his book *Psychic Energy* (Serviere Publishers, Wassenaar, Holland, 1975).

p. 66

Patient with anxiety attacks. Personal communication from Dr. Paul Bick to author.

p. 67

Brain memory. Wilder Penfield, *Mysteries of the Mind* (Princeton University Press, Princeton, N.J., 1975), pp. 21–27.

p. 68

Patient recalling experience of mother at party. Personal communication from Dr. Gary Maier to author.

p. 69

Government reports. "Long Term Effects of Prenatal and Birth Experiences," R. Davies *et al., op cit.*, p. 70.

CHAPTER 4
Intrauterine Bonding

p. 73

Sleeping babies. Stirnimann in Kruse, *op cit.*, p. 52.

p. 74

Brazelton. Reprint of symposium on "Maternal Attachments and Mothering Disorders," sponsored by Johnson & Johnson, Oct. 18–19, 1974, p. 54.

p. 75

Bonding chicks. "Eggs Converse with Hens, Researchers Find," *The New York Times*, July 1, 1980, p. C1.

p. 76

Fetal reaction. E. Reinold, "Vorgeburtliches Verhalten des Feten aus der Sicht des Geburtshelfers," paper read at International Study Society for Prenatal Psychology, September 1979, in Basel, Switzerland.

p. 79

Child rejecting mother. Personal communication from Dr. Peter Fedor-Freybergh.

Schizophrenic mothers. Zax, "Perinatal Characteristics," *op cit.*

Upset mothers. Lester W. Sontag, "Implications of Fetal Behavior and Environment for Adult Personalities," *Annals of New York Academy of Sciences,* pp. 782–786, February 1966.

p. 81

Rubbing stomach. R. Lang at Johnson & Johnson symposium as cited, p. 59.

p. 82

Crying rates. McCall, *op cit.* p. 109.

pp. 83–84

Sound, rock. Clements, *op cit.*

p. 85

Moving stress. Helmut Lukesch, *"Familiare Sozialisation"* (Klett-Cotta, Berlin, 1977), pp. 90–113. See also "Psychosocial Aspects of Pregnancy Counselling," paper delivered by M. Ringler at meeting of International Study Society for Prenatal Psychology, September 1979, in Basel, Switzerland.

Delayed bonding. R.L. Cohen in Marshall Klaus and John Kennell, *Maternal-Infant Bonding* (C.V. Mosby, St. Louis, Mo., 1976), p. 46.

p. 86

Work status. Ringler, *op cit.*

p. 87

Non-randomness of dreams. Milton Kramer *et al.,* "Do Dreams Have Meaning? An Empirical Inquiry," *American Journal of Psychiatry,* pp. 778–781, July 1976.

Dreams and shorter labors. Carolyn Winget and Frederick T. Knapp, "The Relationship of the Manifest Content of Dreams to Duration of labor in Primiparae," *Psychosomatic Medicine,* pp. 313–319, July–August 1972.

p. 89

Abortion and fear of responsibility. J. Joffe in *Prenatal Determinants of Behavior* (Pergamon Press, Oxford, New York, 1969).

p. 90

Abortion and fears of abandonment. R.J. Weil and C. Tupper, "Personality, Life Situation and Communication: A Study of Habitual Abortion," *Psychosomatic Medicine,* 22:6, Nov.–Dec. 1960, pp. 448–455.

p. 91

Emotional thermostat. Ashley Montagu in *Prenatal Influences, op cit.,* pp. 213–214.

p. 92

Dangers of alcohol. "The Fetal Alcohol Syndrome: Alcohol as a Teratogen," *Drug Abuse and Alcoholism Newsletter, vol. 11,* no. 4, May 1978. See also press conference of Dr. Ernest P. Noble, director, U.S. Institute on Alcohol Abuse and Alcoholism, June 2, 1977.

p. 93

Smoking mothers. "Gravida's Smoking Seen Handicap to Offspring," *Obstetrics–Gynecology News,* p. 16, June 15, 1970. See also John F. Murphy *et al,* "The Effect of Age, Parity, and Cigarette Smoking on Baby Weight," *American Journal of Obstetrics & Gynecology,* pp. 22–25, September 1971; G.W. Comstock *et al.,* "Low Birth Weight and Neonatal Mortality Related to Maternal Smoking and Socioeconomic Status," *American Journal of Obstetrics & Gynecology,* pp. 53–59, September 1971.

University of Washington study on caffeine. "Coffee May Perk Up Pregnant Mom but Not Her Baby," *Medical World News,* pp. 12–13, April 17, 1978.

p. 94

Drug taking. Thomas E. O'Brien *et al.,* "Drugs and the Fetus: A Consumer's Guide by Generic and Brand Name," *Birth and Family Journal,* 5:58–86, summer 1978. See also "Present Status of Drugs as Teratogens in Man," *Teratology,* 7:3–16, 1973.

CHAPTER 5
The Birth Experience

p. 98

Radiological studies. Liley, *op cit.,* p. 102.

p. 99

Positioning at birth. David B. Cheek, personal communication to the author.

p. 100

Vaginal *vs.* Caesarean Delivery. Gilbert W. Meier, "Behavior of Infant Monkeys: Differences Attributable to Mode of Birth," *Science,* 143:968–970, 1964.

p. 101

Breech births. News report, *American Journal of Obstetrics & Gynecology,* 1972.

p. 104

Birth and neuropsychiatric disorders. B. Pasamanick and Hilda Knobloch, "Reproductive Studies on the Epidemiology of Reproductive Casualty: Old and New," *Merrill Palmer Quarterly,* 2:7–26, 1966.

Schizophrenia and birth complications. C.N. Rutt and D.R. Offord, "Prenatal and Perinatal Complications in Childhood Schizoprenics and Their Siblings," *Journal of Nervous and Mental Diseases,* 152:321–324, January 1970.

p. 105

Birth as a contributing factor in schizophrenia. Sarnoff A. Mednick, "Breakdown in Individuals at High Risk for Schizophrenia," *Mental Hygiene,* 54:50–61, January 1970.

Violent births and criminality. Sarnoff A. Mednick, "Birth Defects and Schizophrenia," *Psychology Today*, 4 (11):48–50, 80–81, 1971.

p. 107

Laboring times. Reginal P. Lederman *et al.*, "The Relationship of Maternal Anxiety, Plasma Catecholamines, and Plasma Cortisol to Progress in Labor," *American Journal of Obstetrics & Gynecology, 132:* 495–500, November 1, 1970.

Maternal attitudes toward birth. Frederick T. Knapp *et al.*, "Some Psychologic Factors in Prolonged Labor Due to Inefficient Uterine Action," *Comprehensive Psychiatry*, 4:9–17, February 1963.

p. 108

Troubled mothers. Anthony Davids and Spencer DeVault, "Maternal Anxiety During Pregnancy and Childbirth Abnormalities," *Psychosomatic Medicine*, 24:464–469, February 1963.

p. 109

Use of Caesareans, forceps and drugs. John Kelly, "Baby '79: What Every Woman (and Man) Should Know about Childbirth," *Ladies' Home Journal*, pp. 105 and 107, January 1979.

Dangers of drugs. Literally dozens of studies have been done on this subject. Among the most comprehensive of them is a report by Yvonne Brackbill, which Dr. Brackbill included as part of her testimony before the U.S. Senate Subcommittee on Health and Scientific Research, April 17, 1978. See also published testimony of Doris B. Haire on the use of oxytocic drugs for the elective induction of labor before the U.S. Food and Drug Administration, June 21, 1978.

p. 110

Lasting effects of birth injuries. David B. Cheek, "Maladjustment Patterns Apparently Related to Imprinting at Birth," *The American Journal of Clinical Hypnosis*, 18:75–82, October 1975. See also Salam and Adams, *op cit.*, p. 408. These investigators declare flatly: "There can be no doubt that the birth process traumatizes the infant brain."

Migraine patient. Personal communication from Dr. David Cheek to author.

p. 114

Happy children. John Bowlby, "Disruption of Affectional Bonds and Its Effects on Behavior," *Mental Health Supplement, Bimonthly Journal of the* (Canadian) *Department of National Health and Welfare,* Ottawa, January–February 1969.

Bonding. Marshall Klaus and John Kennell, "Maternal Attachment: Importance of the First Post-Partum Days," *The New England Journal of Medicine,* 286:460–463, March 2, 1972.

p. 115

Terrycloth mother. Harry F. Harlow, "Love in Infant Monkeys," *Scientific American,* 200:68–74, June 1959.

CHAPTER 6
The Shaping of Character

p. 120

Edward Bowe. Kelly, *op cit.,* p. 107.

p. 123

Holding. Marc Hollander, "Women's Wish to Be Held: Sexual and Non-Sexual Aspects," *Medical Aspects of Sexuality,* 3:26, April 1973. See also Hollander, "Prostitution, the Body and Human Relations," *International Journal of Psychoanalysis,* 42:404–413, 1961.

Illegitimate pregnancies. C.P. Malinquist *et al.,* "Personality Characteristics of Women with Repeated Illegitimacies: Descriptive Aspects," *American Journal of Orthopsychiatry* 36:476, 1966.

CHAPTER 7
Celebrating Motherhood

p. 127

A typical birth. Michelle Harrison, "Birth as the First Experience of Mothering," in *21st Century Obstetrics and Gynecology Now,* Lee Stewart and David Stewart, editors (NAPSAC, Inc., P. O. Box 267, Marble Hill, Mo. 63764, 1977), pp. 585–587.

p. 130

Body image. Sheila Kitzinger, "Anxiety in Pregnancy," *Journal of Maternal and Child Health,* pp. 358–360, September 1977.

p. 131

Crowded living space. Ringler, *op cit.,* p. 5.

p. 131

Financial responsibilities. Helmut Lukesch, *op cit.,* pp. 103–105.

p. 133

Relationship with husband. Ringler, *op cit.,* p. 4.

Woman's mother. Nils Uddenberg and Carl Frederick Fagerstrom, "The Deliveries of Daughters of Reproductively Maladjusted Mothers," *Journal of Psychosomatic Research,* 20:223–229, 1976.

Woman's fears. Ringler, *op cit.,* p. 2. See also Cohen in Klaus and Kennell, *Maternal-Infant Bonding, op cit.*

p. 134

Birth complications. Marilyn T. Erickson, "The Relationship Between Psychological Variables and Specific Complications of Pregnancy, Labor and Delivery," *Journal of Psychosomatic Research,* 20:207–210, 1976.

p. 142

Leboyer *vs.* gentle birth. Murray Enkin *et al.,* "A Prospective, Randomized Clinical Trial of the Leboyer Approach to Childbirth," unpublished study.

p. 143

Oregon home birth study. Lewis Mehl and David Stewart, "A Rebuttal to Negative Home Birth Statistics Cited by ACOG," in *21st Century Obstetrics, op cit.,* pp. 27–28.

CHAPTER 8
The Vital Bond

p. 148

Mrs. B. Gail Peterson and Lewis Mehl, *Parental/Child Psychology—Delivery Alternatives*, Obtainable from Lewis Mehl, Berkeley, Cal.

Bonding's benefits. Kennell and Klaus, *Maternal-Infant Bonding, op cit.*, pp. 1–15.

Rutgers study. Cited by Dr. Donna K. Kantos in testimony before Canadian Senate's Standing Committee on Health, Welfare, and Science, March 8, 1978. See also Ashley Montagu, *Touching—The Significance of Skin* (second edition, Harper & Row, New York, 1977), p. 28.

p. 149

Child abuse. Dr. Ray Helfer at Johnson & Johnson symposium as cited, pp. 21–25.

Twelve-hour limit. Kennell study cited by Charles Spezzano and Jill Waterman in "The First Day of Life," *Psychology Today*, pp. 110–116, December 1977. See also Kennell at Johnson & Johnson symposium as cited.

p. 150

Diapering and feeding differences. Kennell at Johnson & Johnson symposium as cited, p. 39.

Bonding's universal effect. Montagu, *Touching, op cit.*, pp. 127–149.

p. 152

Stroked babies. Norman Solkoff, "Effects of Handling on the Subsequent Development of Premature Infants," *Developmental Psychology*, 1:765, 1969.

p. 153

IQ study. Kennell at Johnson & Johnson symposium as cited, p. 41.

p. 154

Holding child's attention. Dr. Daniel Stern at Johnson & Johnson symposium as cited, p. 56. See also McCall, *op cit.,* pp. 108–120.

p. 155

Punchline behavior. Stern at Johnson & Johnson symposium as cited, p. 57.

p. 157

Breastfeeding: Seattle study. N.W. Johnson, "Breastfeeding in the First Hour of Life," *American Journal of Maternal-Child Nursing* (1):12–16, 1976.

Brazilian study. Cited by Klaus and Kennell in "Early Mother-Infant Contact," *Bulletin Menninger Clinic,* 43:93, 1979.

p. 158

Wisconsin study on fathers. Ross Parke at Johnson & Johnson symposium as cited, p. 61.

Engrossment. M. Greenberg and N. Morris, "Engrossment: The Newborn's Impact on the Father," *American Journal of Orthopsychiatry,* 44:520–531, 1974.

p. 159

Sex differences in play. Glenn Collins, "A New Look at Life with Father, *The New York Times Magazine,* June 17, 1979, p. 50.

p. 160

Brazelton, *Ibid,* p. 52

p. 161

Separation protest. *Ibid.,* p. 50

CHAPTER 9
The First Year

p. 165

Vision. McCall, *op cit.,* p. 53.

p. 166

Adult Voices. Stern quoted at Johnson & Johnson symposium as cited, p. 56. See also McCall, *op cit.,* pp. 55–56.

Maternal smell. Macfarlane in McCall, *op cit.,* p. 58.

Infant personality. Alexander Thomas, Stella Chess and R.G. Birch, "The Origins of Personality," *Scientific American,* August 1970.

p. 169

Tickling as a social act. Burton White, *The First Three Years of Life* (Prentice-Hall, Englewood Cliffs, N.J., 1975), p. 50.

p. 170

Infant memory. Friedman in McCall, *op cit.,* p. 83.

p. 171

Feeding schedule. McCall, *op cit.,* p. 84.

Mimic. Andrew N. Meltzoff and M. Keith Moore, "Imitation of Facial and Manual Gestures by Human Neonates," *Science,* 198:75–78, October 7, 1977.

p. 173

Sensitive mother. Mary Ainsworth *et al.,* "Individual Differences in Strange-Situation Behavior of One-Year-Olds," in *Origins of Human Relations,* H.R. Schaffer, editor (Academic Press, New York, 1974), pp. 17–52.

p. 177

Crying and seeing differences between baby girls and boys. Maggie Scarf, "Women and Depression," *New Republic,* pp. 25–29, July 5, 1980.

Male and female emotional characteristics. "Cognitive Differences in Sexes," *Psychiatric News,* January 4, 1980.

p. 178

Piaget. McCall, *op cit.,* p. 98.

p. 179

Infant's reaction to strangers. *Ibid.*, pp. 125–128.

p. 181

Learning of simple phrases. Burton White, "The Critical Importance of Hearing," *The Center for Parent Education Newsletter*, p. 2, June 1979.

Brightest toddlers. Burton White, Harvard Pre-school Project, The Center for Parent Education, Newton, Mass.

CHAPTER 10
Retrieving Early Memories

p. 186

Oxytocin. Bela Bohus *et al.*, "Oxytocin, Vasopressin and Memory: Opposite Effects on Consolidation and Retrieval Processes," *Brain Research*, 157:414–417, 1978.

p. 187

ACTH. J. Kastin *et al.*, "The Effects of MSH and MIF on the Brain," in *Autonomical Neuroendocrinology*, W.E. Stumpf and L.D. Grant, editors (Kroger, 1975).

pp. 187–88

State dependent learning. D.A. Overton, "State Dependent or Disassociated Learning Produced with Pentobarbital," *Journal of Comparative and Physiological Psychology*, 57:3–12, 1964. See also D.R. Meyer, "Access to Engrams," *American Psychologist*, 27:124–133, 1972; A.H. Black, N.J. Carlson and R.I. Solomon, "Exploratory Study of the Conditioned Responses in Curarized Dogs," *Psychological Monographs*, 1962.

CHAPTER 11
Society and the Unborn Child

p. 195

Fetal growth. Robert Rugg and Landrum B. Shettles, *From Conception to Birth* (Harper & Row, New York, 1974.), p. 61.

p. 196

Harvard criteria. Bernard Nathanson, *Aborting America* (Doubleday & Co., Garden City, N.Y., 1979), p. 165.

p. 197

Abortion studies. Marlene Hunter, "Applications for Abortion at a Community Hospital," *Canadian Medical Association Journal,* pp. 1088–1092, Nov. 16, 1974; Eloise Jones, "A Psychiatrist's Experience with Legal Abortion in Canada," in *Death Before Birth,* E.J. Kremer and E.A. Synan, editors (Griffin House, Toronto, 1974), pp. 177–186.

p. 198

Sex selection. John Elliott, "Abortion for Wrong Fetal Sex: An Ethical Legal Dilemma," *Journal of the American Medical Association,* 242 (12):1455–1456, October 5, 1979.

p. 199

Emotional consequences of abortion. W. Cates *et al.,* "Regulation of Abortion Services—For Better or Worse," *The New England Journal of Medicine,* pp. 720–723, September 27, 1979; Colin Brewer, "Incidence of Post-Abortion Psychosis: A Prospective Study," *British Medical Journal,* pp. 476–477, February 19, 1977.

p. 202

Obstetrical battleground. Franklin quoted by Kelly in "Baby '79," p. 105.

p. 211

Russian adoption rate. Klaus and Kennell, *Maternal-Infant Bonding, op cit.,* p. 111.

Stanford study. *Ibid.,* p. 104.

p. 212

Visiting practices. *Ibid.,* p. 116.

Sources of
Further Information

Books

Arms, Suzanne, *Immaculate Deception.*, Houghton Mifflin Co., Boston, 1975. Describes how hospitals complicate childbirth, compares childbirth practices in other countries, presents a strong argument for home birth. A feminist point of view.

Bean, Constance. *Methods of Childbirth.* Doubleday & Co., Garden City, N.Y., 1972. Excellent general guide for choosing hospital, doctor, childbirth classes, drugs and so on. Encourages consumers to exercise their options as adults rather than as patients.

Berends, Polly Berrien. *Whole Child, Whole Person.* Harper & Row, New York, 1975. An almanac of stimulations, theoretical and practical for parents. The author provides many creative activities that parents and children can share.

Brazelton, T. Berry. *Infants and Mothers.* Dell Publishing Co., New York, 1969. Guide to normal developmental stages.

Brewer, Gail Sforza (ed.), *The Pregnancy After 30 Workbook.* Rodale Press, Emmaus, Pa., 1978.

Brewer, Gail Sforza, and Brewer, Tom. *What Every Pregnant Woman Should Know: The Truth About Diets and Drugs in Pregnancy.* Penguin Books, New York, 1979.

Briggs, Dorothy Corkille. *Your Child's Self-Esteem.* Doubleday Dolphin Books, Garden City, N.Y., 1977. Step-by-step

233

guidelines for raising children with a healthy mentality and strong ego.

Elkins, Valmai Howe. *The Rights of the Pregnant Parent.* Waxwing Productions, Toronto; Two Continents, New York, 1976; new edition, 1980. Stresses good prenatal care and optimal obstetrical care. Very consumer-oriented.

Grof, Stanislav. *Realms of the Human Unconscious.* E.P. Dutton, New York, 1976. In this book Grof describes the results of his nearly two decades of pioneering drug research. His case histories show the many ways in which the mind can transcend the narrow confines of ego. Highly recommended for those interested in the more spiritual, mystical or transpersonal aspects of being.

Kitzinger, Sheila. *The Experience of Childbirth,* 3rd edition. G. Nichols & Co., Great Britain, 1974. British author emphasizes the harmony of the body with feelings and emotions; discusses importance of the pelvic floor release during birth.

———. *The Experience of Breastfeeding.* Penguin Books, New York, 1979.

Klaus, Marshall H., and Kennell, John H. *Maternal-Infant Bonding.* C.V. Mosby Co., St. Louis, 1976. This is the authoritative text on the subject. Easy to read yet rigorously scientific.

Laing, R.D. *The Facts of Life.* Pantheon Books, New York, 1976. This is a brilliant, often perplexing but always stimulating book. Laing, by referring to his own life, clinical case histories and various myths speculates on the extent to which our prenatal and birth experience may resonate in us through our entire lives.

Leboyer, Frederick. *Birth Without Violence.* Alfred A. Knopf, New York, 1976. The book that started the obstetrical revolution producing a more gentle, humane type of birth. Poetic and controversial.

McCall, Robert. *Infants: The New Knowledge.* Harvard University Press, Cambridge, Mass., 1979. An intelligent guide to the child's first years, both informative and entertaining.

NAPSAC publications available from NAPSAC, Marble Hill,

Mo.: *Safe Alternatives in Childbirth,* 1976; *21st Century Obstetrics Now,* vols. 1 & 2, 1977. *Compulsory Hospitalization/Freedom of Choice in Childbirth,* vols. 1, 2 & 3, 1979.

Nathanson, Bernard N. *Aborting America.* Doubleday & Co., Garden City, N.Y., 1979. The most thorough review of the subject available to date. The author is a well-known obstetrician who, in spite of his personal bias against abortion, reviews fairly and thoroughly all the arguments for and against it. Must reading for anyone who is professionally concerned with this issue.

Noble, Elizabeth. *Essential Exercises for the Childbearing Year.* Houghton Mifflin Co., Boston, 1976. Straightforward, practical guide for both the pre- and post-delivery period.

Osofsky, Joy D. *Handbook of Infant Development.* John Wiley & Sons, New York, 1979. This book will be of more interest to academicians. It contains a great amount of clinical research and statistical analysis, but it also provides a tremendous amount of information on the psychology of infancy from the traditional point of view.

White, Burton, *The First Three Years of Life.* Prentice-Hall, Englewood Cliffs, N.J., 1978.

Journals & Periodicals

American Mother Magazine. Subscription address: P.O. Box 2549, Boulder, Col. 80321. *American Mother* is a monthly magazine designed to popularize the ideals of enlightened childbirth and the family life movement. It is available on newsstands and in supermarkets, as well as by subscription.

Birth and the Family Journal. 110 El Camino Real, Berkeley, Cal. 94705. A consumer/medical journal quarterly, it features full-length reviews of the medical literature on specific topics and original research reports. Regular features include an index and abstract of the current medical literature and film and book reviews.

Birthing Newsletter. P.O. Box 415, Winona Lake, Ind. 46590. A monthly newsletter intended for both childbirth educators and parents; provides current information on childbirth and obstetrics.

The Federal Monitor. Ann Gray, Drawer Q., McLean, Va. 22101. *The Federal Monitor* is an excellent periodical that keeps its subscribers posted on current legislative and legal activities likely to affect the health care of women and children.

Mothering. P.O. Box 2046, Albuquerque, N.M. 87103. *Mothering* is a quarterly magazine that covers all aspects of natural childbirth, pregnancy, post-natal care and family health.

The NAPSAC News. P.O. Box 267, Marble Hill, Mo. 63764. *The NAPSAC News,* which publishes quarterly and is available to NAPSAC members, keeps readers up to date on all the important current issues in the childbirth reform movement. It is a valuable resource for parents and educators.

National Health Directory. 6410 Rochledge Dr., Suite 208, Bethesda, Md. 20034. The 1980 edition lists the names of more than 19,000 key health/medical officials currently serving on the national and local levels.

The People's Doctor Newsletter. 664 North Michigan Ave., Suite 720, Chicago, Ill. 60611. Edited by Robert Mendelsohn, M.D. *The People's Doctor Newsletter* is a bimonthly medical newsletter for consumers. Each issue highlights a specific medical area and follows a question-and-answer format in discussing major topics. Each issue contains a column by Marian Tompson, one of the founding mothers of La Leche League International.

Women and Health. Biological Sciences Program. State University of New York at Old Westbury, Old Westbury, N.Y. 11568. A bimonthly academic journal, *Women and Health* focuses on issues in women's health care delivery, women as health workers, female physiology and women's medical care. Regular features include Women, Health and the Law; Women, Health and Books; and Women, Health and Work.

Films

Cinema Medica, 2325 West Foster, Chicago, Ill. 60625. Cinema Medica has more than 25 films in most areas of childbirth—family-centered hospitals, home birth, birth centers, caesarean surgery, nutrition in pregnancy, children at birth and so on. Available in 16mm, super 8 and video cassette, for sale and rental.

City Films Distribution Ltd., 376 Wellington Ave. West, Toronto, Ontario. A very large library of birth and child development films, including Leboyer's *Birth Without Violence.* Anything they don't carry, they can usually get for you.

Ages and Stage Series. This series of 6 films, produced in the 1950s, was the first modern attempt to present on film a study of child behavior at various age levels, and provide stage-by-stage guidance about what children need from parents. The films are entitled "He Acts His Age," "The Terrible Twos and Trusting Threes," "The Frustrating Fours and the Fascinating Fives," "From Sociable Six to Noisy Nine," "From Ten to Twelve" and "The Teens". All these films are available from The National Film Board of Canada. *United States:* 1251 Ave. of the Americas, New York, N.Y. 10020. *Canada:* P.O.B. 6100, Station A, Montreal, Quebec H3C 3H5, or 150 Kent St., Ottawa, Ontario K1A OM9.

"Footsteps" is a television series on parenting; it focuses on some of the problems and concerns that all parents of young children face. Distributor: National Audiovisual Center, General Services Administration, Washington, D.C. 20409, Attn.: Reference Section.

"Look at Me" is a parent-education program developed by WTTW (Chicago) and Parents Are Resources, a group devoted to helping parents realize various ways they can stimulate their child's development without having to purchase expensive toys. This series was aired on WTTW-TV and is now distributed by Perennial Education, Inc., 1825 Willow Rd., P.O.B. 236, Northfield, Ill. 60093.

Resources

The American Academy of Husband-Coached Childbirth. P.O. Box 5224, Sherman Oaks, Cal. 91413 (Bradley method).

American College of Home Obstetrics, c/o Gregory White, M.D., 2821 Rose St., Franklin Park, Ill. 60131.

The American College of Nurse-Midwives, 100 Vermont Ave. N.W., Washington, D.C. 20005.

American Fertility Society, 1608 Thirteenth Ave. S., Suite 101, Birmingham, Ala. 35205.

America Foundation for Maternal and Child Health, Inc., 30 Beekman Pl., New York, N.Y. 10022.

American Society of Psychoprophylaxis in Obstetrics (ASPO), 1523 L Street N.W., Washington, D.C. 20005 (Lamaze method).

Center for Parent Education, 55 Chapel St., Newton, Mass. 02160. Director: Burton L. White, Ph.D. A public service organization offering the following services and products to professionals concerned with the education of children in the first three years of life:

> Advisory service on materials for education for parent-hood activities including assessment techniques, curricula and any other material under consideration
> Consultation on research and service programs offered here and on site
> Audio-visual materials for training staff and parents
> Personnel guidance
> Basic and applied research
> Conference presentations by specialists in education for parenthood

C-SEC Inc., Cesarian Support, Education and Concern, Inc., 66 Christopher St., Waltham, Mass. 02154.

H.O.M.E. (Home Oriented Maternity Experience), 511 New York Ave., Takoma Park, Washington, D.C. 20012.

I.C.E.A. (International Childbirth Education Association), P.O. Box 20852, Milwaukee, Wisc. 53220.

La Leche League International, 9616 Minneapolis Ave., Franklin Park, Ill. 60131 (Breastfeeding).

Maternity Center Association, 48 East 92nd St., New York, N.Y. 10028 (first maternity center in the U.S.).

NAPSAC (National Association of Parents and Professionals for Safe Alternatives in Childbirth), P.O. Box 276, Marble Hill, Mo. 63764 (David and Lee Stewart).

National Foundation of the March of Dimes Genetic Counseling Centers, 1275 Mamaroneck Ave., White Plains, N.Y. 10605.

Society for the Protection of the Unborn Through Nutrition, Suite 603, 17 North Wabash Ave., Chicago, Ill. 60602 (Dr. Tom Brewer).

The National Center for Clinical Infant Programs, P.O. Box 73, Glen Echo, Md. 20768 (Eleanor Szanton, Executive Director). The National Center, established in the summer of 1977, is a non-profit tax-exempt corporation, designed "to facilitate mental health through preventive clinical approaches in the earliest years of life, to provide and to foster the development of information and public policy in this important and emerging field."

England

The National Childbirth Trust, 9 Queensborough Terrace, Bayswater, London, W.2.

La Leche Great Britain, Box 3424, London W.C.1 6XX.

Canada

CEA (Childbirth Education Association), 33 Price St., Toronto, Ontario, M4W 1Z2 (local chapters throughout Canada).

LCAO, Lamaze Childbirth Association of Ontario, 136 Douglas Ave., Toronto, Ontario M5M 1G6.

Index